AFRICA
BETWEEN EAST AND WEST

Africa
Between East and West

A BACKGROUND BOOK

John Dumoga

DUFOUR

© John W. K. Dumoga 1969
Published in the U.S. by
Dufour Editions Inc.
Chester Springs, Pennsylvania 19425
Library of Congress Catalog Card number: 76–77360
Manufactured in Great Britain
First published in the U.S.A. 1969

CONTENTS

Introduction

THE PURPOSE OF this book is primarily to examine some of the problems confronting the leaders and peoples in post-independence Africa, south of the Sahara—problems of nationalism, the ideological struggle between the salesmen of East and West for the control of the continent, and effects of this struggle on the policies of various African countries, the search for democracy and unity on the continent, and the implications of the new concept of African socialism—and to suggest some solutions to these problems.

Naturally, there are no easy solutions. In the final analysis, it is for each country or nation-state to find its own solutions in the light of its historical and present circumstances, while keeping in mind all the time the ultimate welfare of its own nationals.

Can the leaders of independent African countries solve these problems by blaming foreigners and 'neo-colonialists' for their mistakes? Can they continue blaming outsiders for the failure of their ill-conceived policies? Can they successfully persuade their nationals to continue making sacrifices for ever, with the dubious hope of inheriting a greater, better and happier tomorrow?

Experience has shown that the answers to some of these questions can only be in the negative, particularly in countries where the people have waited for some time for the various governments to satisfy their rising expectations without much success.

I am, however, convinced that the battle for survival is not yet totally lost, provided African leaders do not lose sight of their ultimate goals, namely the dignity of the human being and the welfare of their nationals.

In our endeavour to reach these goals we must learn not to blame foreigners for our shortcomings and failures, as has been the style in too many countries of late, but to face our own problems with courage and dignity, and work out effective solutions to them.

Mr Robert K. Gardiner, Ghanaian Executive Secretary of the Economic Commission for Africa, in a speech to the East African Women's seminar at Kabete, Kenya, on April 17, 1964, warned against this easy way out of African troubles in these words:

'I am convinced that the almost perpetual moaning about neo-colonialism and foreign intrigues is harmful to national morale. We must live and act as persons sufficiently matured and capable of protecting our own interests. Diatribes against broken pledges are the claptrap of minor politicians. The most serious aspect of the technique of accusing foreigners or the Opposition when official policies fail is that it might provide a smokescreen to hide the faults of governments. Moreover, the tendency to see oneself perpetually as a victim will lead to the evasion of responsibility and condoning of evil.

'There is a lot to be done to develop our economies, to provide facilities for the enrichment of life and to catch up with the technologically advanced countries, but this should not be done as part of life. We should avoid being caught in the net of never-ending preparations and plans. This temptation is created at a time when officials and politicians remain inexperienced and work under pressure from so many outside salesmen. As a Russian writer puts it, "Man is born to live, not to prepare for life"'.

After nearly a decade of independence, African leaders must now be prepared to take further steps forward towards giving their nationals the opportunities necessary for living a fuller life. This book discusses some of the necessary steps in this direction.

J. W. K. Dumoga

Accra, Ghana, August, 1968

I
Promises Prior to Independence

A PROPHET OF doom, Drew Middleton of the *New York Times*, confidently predicted, after a tour of fifteen African countries in May, 1966: 'Five to ten years of coups, revolutions and turmoil in general probably lie ahead for black Africa's independent nations as they telescope twenty centuries of political and economic development into twenty years.'[1]

On closer examination it can be seen that the turmoil, coups and revolutions predicted by this perceptive journalist were not conjured out of his fertile imagination, but from a careful observation and analysis of the African political scene in the middle of 1966.

Independent African States have had nearly a decade to manage or mismanage their own affairs, and yet all the indications are that coups, revolutions and turmoil still lie ahead of some of them. What are the reasons for this state of affairs?

In West Africa, the battle-cry during the struggle for independence was 'freedom' or '*ablode*' and its equivalent in the various indigenous tribal languages. In the Congo, it was 'independence', and in East Africa it was '*uhuru*'. During this exercise to cast off the colonial yoke African leaders have had to develop their concepts and language to reflect their dependent status. Thus the real issues of independence were, perhaps, over-simplified. During the period of the colonial struggle few political leaders in any country had the time, the foresight, the courage, and very few the honesty, to tell their countrymen and women, the ordinary citizens, the real implications of independence.

[1] For Reference Notes see p. 132.

Very few leaders are on record for having told their compatriots that independence did not mean, for instance, taking over, without compensation, the white colonial master's house, farms, mines, timber concessions and mansions; that independence meant harder work and sometimes more privation for the citizens. Very few, if any, of the leaders who headed the independence struggle were far-seeing enough to remind their fellow colonial subjects that after independence all the money that would be needed for financing development projects—the hospitals, schools, clinics, new community halls, roads, ports and harbours promised them—would have to come mostly from their own tax moneys, the sweat and toil of their own efforts. Very few politicians took the trouble to remind their peoples that independence would place squarely on their own shoulders the responsibility of lifting themselves up by their own bootstraps so as to achieve and enjoy the life abundant promised them.

It is also a matter of historical record that during the elections that preceded independence, freedom or *uhuru*, the thought uppermost in almost everybody's mind was the termination of the colonial era—a legitimate expression of the will of the people to withdraw from foreign domination—so as to become masters in their own houses in their own countries. Thus on the eve of independence not many of us associated the vital process of electing a government with powers of life and death; we had no idea that this election process—placing a piece of paper in a ballot box carrying the picture of a red cockerel as in Ghana and Kenya—would give our own African brothers, the new rulers, powers to enact inimical laws such as Preventive Detention Acts or powers to change the constitutions agreed upon between all the political parties before independence.

After independence most African electors found to their dismay, keen disappointment and, more often than not, horror that by the simple act of casting their votes for their fellow men and women, they had given them power to make laws to control everything, including their very lives. Many

ordinary citizens who did not know it before have found out
to their chagrin and bitter disappointment that they became
free from colonial domination only to land in another slave
camp, this time managed by their own kith and kin. Ordinary African citizens in the new States found to their disappointment that they had indeed been liberated from
colonial rule, but had not yet earned the freedom which was
promised them during the struggle for independence.

The Atlantic Charter, signed by President Roosevelt and
Prime Minister Churchill in mid-Atlantic during World War
II, was one of the basic documents which inspired colonial
freedom. The two leaders hardly reached their home ports
before Dr Nnamdi Azikiwe of Nigeria sent cablegrams to
the Colonial Office in London asking whether the Atlantic
Charter proclaiming the Four Freedoms applied to Nigeria
also. The leaders of the independence struggle kept before
them the promises inscribed in the Atlantic Charter during
the whole period of the struggle for independence. They
quoted freely from this historic document, promising their
fellow citizens the Four Freedoms and much more. It was
made abundantly clear that after the colonial masters had
relinquished their power the African would gain not only
political and economic power but every other advantage that
had been denied him under the colonial regimes. Former
President Nkrumah of Ghana perhaps put it vividly when
he said: 'Seek ye first the political kingdom and everything
else shall be added unto you.'

During the struggle for independence the politicians, particularly those in West Africa, took great care to define what
they meant by 'everything else' which would be added to
freedom from colonial rule. These things include the building of new mansions, super highways, hospitals and clinics
in all parts of the country, electric power plants for lights in
every village hut and for industrialisation, schools, and other
institutions of higher learning, higher prices for cash crops
and control of the mineral and natural resources and their

exploitation by the people's own government for the benefit of the ordinary citizen and his government.

These promises of the shape of things to come were not dissimilar to those made by European statesmen prior to the end of World War II. War-weary Europeans were promised: 'Peace would begin, everything would begin again—holidays, leisure-trips, pleasure, maybe even happiness, but certainly freedom.'

Similarly, African political leaders who spearheaded the independence struggle had to set their goals high so as to get their message of deliverance across to their largely illiterate and apathetic fellow citizens. But the important distinction which the leaders failed to draw was that between *freedom* and *happiness*. Our experiences after the attainment of independence have underscored clearly this distinction. In certain countries some of the leaders became *happy*, according to their own lights and the material wealth they have managed to acquire. The majority of this happy breed of men and women are leaders who suddenly found themselves in positions of power, and did not disdain to use this power in acquiring great wealth for themselves and their immediate dependants and political hangers-on. In this process of amassing wealth the new leaders lost sight of the original purpose of the independence struggle, namely the freedom of all the people in the new States, and not just the happiness of the top stratum of society.

Events during the past two or three years have amply demonstrated that it is this equation of happiness for the few top leaders with the freedom for the many that is mainly responsible for the coups, revolutions and turmoil in the new States.

One of the primary causes of political discord is that independence has failed to solve the problems of the new African States and, in most cases, has added new ones. And the gap between the top political leadership in all countries without exception, created by the unbridled greed and avidity for wealth by the leadership themselves in terms of material welfare, has added insult to injury and is one of the chief causes of political discontent in all the new States. Besides, events during the past few years have demonstrated that in many instances, with few exceptions, the leaders of the struggle for independence are unsuited for the routine, drab, day-to-day details of running a government or of making a backward economy work efficiently.

In their struggle to solve or tackle intelligently the problems of independence some African leaders, knowing that they could not, in clear conscience, attribute their failures to the departed colonialists, have created new bogeymen—neo-colonialism and neo-imperialism—whom they blame for everything. This new tactic does not go down well with the ordinary citizens. These ordinary citizens, who had been convinced, persuaded or fooled long before independence to expect great improvements in their living conditions, have tended to blame the leaders when they have seen that the promised improvements have not materialised or when they see that their living standards are falling or have already fallen.

This reaction from the ordinary citizens must be expected. These ordinary citizens seek to live and rightly expect the leaders of the new States to help them to make life possible and full. They tend to be disappointed when the leaders evade this responsibility or hide behind adolescent fantasies such as neo-colonialism, transitional periods, worlds-in-the-making, growing-pains and subversive activities of foreign spies as ends in themselves.

The disappointments of the ordinary citizens are also aggravated by the authoritarianism of too many governments of the new States. African politicians often tell their fellow countrymen and women that affairs of State are so serious and complex that ordinary citizens should not expect to understand them. This is not true. This assumption that only those in government can understand the basic issues about running a country, that only political leaders have wisdom, is partly responsible for the popularity of the one-party

States that proliferate on the continent. It is the same assumption which has become the midwife of the numerous coups, revolutions and turmoil on the continent. Most political leaders have lost sight of the Akan proverb which says 'Ti koro nko agyina'—one head does not hold counsel.

Mr Robert K. Gardiner, whom I have already quoted in my Introduction, perhaps had this in mind when, in that same 1964 speech, he asked Africans to develop curiosity about government policies and actions. He suggested that ordinary citizens should put five questions to each proposal put forward by public leaders in every country in the new States of Africa, namely:

(a) What is the Government doing?
(b) Why is it doing it?
(c) How is it setting about it?
(d) What results does the Government expect; and
(e) Within what period of time?

These questions were surely designed to emphasise the importance of public curiosity, without which any government could easily cease to be accountable to the community. Dr K. A. Busia puts the problem of curiosity and its effect on democratic society in these words: 'There can be no true democracy where there is no free expression of opinion in public affairs or criticism of the ruling body.' Any member of the community could take part in the public discussions of community affairs, or in the public hearings and 'anyone —even the most ordinary youth—will offer his opinion, or make a suggestion with an equal chance of its being heard as if it proceeded from the most experienced sage'.[2]

This public curiosity, exercised by 'even the most ordinary youth', as Brodie Cruickshank observed in the Gold Coast in the nineteenth century, is part and parcel of the African traditional method of discussion and compromise, but appears to have been sadly abandoned by the new leaders of Africa today. In every country most leaders in all spheres of life are so involved in organising societies, movements, co-operatives, trades unions and even political parties or groups that they often mistake such institutions for the ends which they are ultimately intended to serve. But close examinations of this involvement will reveal that the only end of such activities is the fuller and richer life of the citizen—the life which Nigerian politicians called during the independence struggle 'the life abundant'.

This appears to be the sole reason why we must concern ourselves in every African country with poverty, disease, ignorance, high mortality rates, the welfare of the disabled and the handicapped. The under-privileged sections of the community everywhere in Africa are denied opportunities for the more abundant life. These under-privileged people must be recognised as a responsibility of all leaders and the State. Any other interpretation of the ends which the State must serve, especially the popular view which regards the State as an end to be served by an unquestioning populace, is not only false but extremely dangerous, as the various coups, revolutions and turmoil have so far amply demonstrated.

The people and Government make up the State everywhere in the world.

When enlightened or even ordinary citizens dare to outline the rights or entitlements of their fellow citizens—all of them—to contribute to the solution of the problems and the provision of facilities, they do not do so out of spite or because they are necessarily 'violent, waspish and malignant'[3] and therefore to be silenced through the employment of 'temporary measures of benevolent dictatorship'.[4] They do so because they have no wish to abdicate their right to openly participate in public discussions of such issues as they know they have a stake in the general welfare of the people, but above all in their own personal welfare and betterment.

Most citizens do not believe, as in the past in certain countries, that it is sufficient to point out deficiencies, failures and faults in criticising the departed colonialists or the new bogeymen, neo-colonialism or neo-imperialism, but believe that Africans must now recognise their own deficiencies and decide to take action to make good or remove them, and they believe genuinely that such remedial action can only be taken through open discussion leading in turn to political action.

As is to be expected, leaders of the new African States are trying to fulfil pre-independence promises to their peoples not only through political action, the ultimate weapon, but also through pragmatic action in the economic and social fields at home and cultural and technical arrangements at the international level. In all these endeavours our leaders have had to develop new concepts or adapt the age-old concepts of both Eastern and Western Europeans to fit their particular circumstances. For instance, most African governments have accepted in principle the liberal democratic ideas of Western Europe which they believe are useful in the establishment of democratic societies, ideas which guarantee human dignity, ideas which make for racial equality and harmony.

In the economic field the new States have accepted in principle the need for economic planning or what some call 'command economies' on the pattern of the Eastern European bloc because they believe that it is largely through such planning that they could make any sense or progress out of the chaotic economies inherited from the colonial exploiters and prevent further exploitation of their fellow citizens by new capitalists, both home-grown ones and foreign operators. President Julius Nyerere of Tanzania expressed this view clearly in his famous address on *Ujamaa: The Basis of African Socialism*, at Kivukoni College in Dar-es-Salaam in April, 1962, when he said that *Ujamaa*, or familyhood, is 'opposed to capitalism which seeks to build a happy society on the basis of the exploitation of man by man'.[5]

In their relations with other countries, the new States have adopted policies of 'non-alignment and positive neutralism' to govern their dealings with the protagonists of Eastern and Western brands of democracy in the hope that they would be spared the heartaches and contortions of the Cold War and at the same time remain free to contribute their own ideas and philosophies to the conduct of international relations, particularly at the level of the United Nations.

Efforts have been and are still being made to forge closer links with fellow African countries through such continental bodies as the Organisation for African Unity, the *Conseil de L'Entente* of West Africa, the OCAM of Francophone States, the various Economic Communities, the African Development Bank and similar regional bodies.

We shall discuss some of the trends that have emerged in the new States during the past few years; analyse some of the problems and the methods used by African leaders to solve them and forecast, if possible, the shape of events to come in certain areas.

We live in a world of peoples. For this reason we have to deal with people from both East and West in the conduct of our domestic and external affairs. Ideas of both East and West have impinged themselves, for good and evil, on the developments of events in Africa. We cannot, however, escape our responsibilities by hiding behind the results of this clash of cultures, inter-action of ideas and peoples, to justify our achievements and failures. We have, as a people, to remember always that independence has created new problems, radically changed our values in certain areas beyond all recognition, while in other areas values have remained almost static or been barely touched by the winds of *Uhuru*.

Our experiences of the pre-independence era do not provide sufficient guidance or reassurances for the solutions of all these problems. At the same time we are already preparing the way to the future.

The imperative need then, it appears to me, is to guard against the wholesale, unquestioning acceptance of certain ideas from the propagandists of both East and West. We need to examine our circumstances, set our goals and targets according to our historical circumstances and go forward to

17

reach our destinations. In this forward march towards our targets we must endeavour to remember always that there are no easy, tailor-made solutions to our problems, nor can there ever be any. We cannot ignore reality and hide behind slogans in the false hope that we can provide ourselves or our children with prefabricated salvation.

2
African Socialism in Action—I

I HAVE SAID that independence has not brought any substantial betterment in the conditions of life to the majority of ordinary citizens in the new States of Africa, and that the promises of the nationalist leaders have yet to be fulfilled.

One doctrine that has guided and continues to influence the actions and policies of leaders in the new States is African socialism. There is yet to be an agreed definition of what exactly African socialism connotes. There are also differences in the degree of emphasis placed on the various aspects of African socialism in the various countries. This is to be expected since the doctrine is barely ten years old and the exponents of the concept are still struggling to define it. However, there are certain characteristics of African socialism that are clearly recognisable in every country.

African socialism is a vigorous child born out of the conflict of ideas and reaction of African thinkers and leaders to colonialism, communism, the democratic ideas of the West, capitalism and the centuries-old kinship and communal ideas and practices of Africans themselves. As a compound of these ingredients, it is difficult to define the doctrine sharply and pretend that such a definition is acceptable to all exponents of the doctrine in the new States of Africa. In these circumstances what is essential is not the exact definition of the doctrine, but the realisation and appreciation of the fact that it works for African leaders and that it is being applied with varying degrees of success and failure in the solution of the complex post-independence problems of economic development and reconstruction, Pan-Africanism, internationalism, the search for democracy and the agonising search for a fresh approach towards maintenance of human dignity and racial harmony.

Leon Trotsky once wrote that 'revolutions are always verbose'. So it is with the African revolution of the 1960s. Since the concept of African socialism became fashionable nearly a decade ago, thousands of words have been written about it; many scholars and exponents have struggled to define it, and many more have criticised and condemned it as an unacceptable, unrealistic philosophy, unworthy of consideration by the orthodox socialists of both East and West. Our concern here is to examine how the doctrine has been used as a guiding principle by African political leaders to solve their problems in various fields, how successful they have been and how miserably they have failed in other fields. We shall also examine some of the criticisms voiced by the so-called orthodox socialists, particularly those of the East and some of their African disciples, and find out how far the concept has deviated from orthodox Marxist-Leninist teachings and what are the effects of this deviation from orthodoxy on the fortunes of African States.

Despite the absence of an acceptable or generally agreed definition of African socialism, coupled with the reluctance of certain African Heads of State to be identified as 'socialists', there are at least five themes clearly discernible in the doctrine and practice of African socialism. These are:

(i) African socialism and its application to economic development;

(ii) African socialism and promotion of Pan-Africanism;

(iii) African socialism and conduct of international relations;

(iv) African socialism and the growth of one-party states; and

(v) African socialism and the confrontation with Eastern and Western democracies.

Let us briefly examine the practice of African leaders in each of these fields and see how far the new States have succeeded or failed in the application of the doctrine towards the solution of post-independence problems.

Economic Development and Reconstruction

It is perhaps in the field of economic planning and development that African leaders and exponents of African socialism have been most articulate, emphatic and precise in their thinking. Colonialism bequeathed mainly monocultural economies to most of the new States, based mainly on the production of cash-crops such as cocoa, coffee, tea, sisal, groundnuts and bananas. By some curious coincidence, the prices of these commodities were fairly high on world markets on the eve of independence, so much so that some of the colonial territories were able barely to balance their budgets. Either by design or accident, the prices of these same commodities dropped sharply immediately after the attainment of independence by the various colonies while the prices of manufactured goods from the metropolitan countries rose sharply out of all proportion to the prices of the raw materials from the newly independent countries. The result was that the economies of these new States were completely disrupted and the new leaders found themselves unable to implement successfully their ambitious economic and social development plans and fulfil the promises made to their peoples for the more abundant life on attainment of independence.

Confronted with these harsh economic realities of independence, most African leaders searched for quick and effective solutions. Some turned to the methods of centrally-planned economies of Eastern Europe; some relied heavily on financial aid from their ex-colonial masters to balance their budgets, while others relied on the new doctrine of African socialism and its traditional elements familiar to the experiences of their nationals as the key to the solution of their economic problems.

For various historical, economic and social reasons, most African leaders have equated economic planning with the concept of African socialism and have sought to gear their centrally-planned economies to the teachings of the doctrine.

The exponents of the doctrine have laid emphasis on various aspects of their concept but have differed in their application. In order to appreciate the differences between the various theories and practices of the general concept, it will be necessary to examine briefly what is happening in several East and West African countries. I hope that such an examination would throw some further light on what the concept means in these new States.

Tanzanian African Socialism

President Julius Nyerere of Tanzania is the most eloquent exponent of African socialism in East Africa. He defined his concept of the doctrine as far back as 1962 in his now famous Kivukoni College address in Dar-es-Salaam and laid much emphasis on what he described as familyhood or *ujamaa* as the cornerstone of the doctrine of African socialism. President Nyerere said in the course of that address:

> 'Our first step, therefore, must be to re-educate ourselves; to regain our former attitude of mind. In our traditional African society we were individuals within a community. We took care of the community, and the community took care of us. We neither needed nor wished to exploit our fellow men.
>
> 'In rejecting the capitalist attitude of mind which colonialism brought into Africa we must reject also the capitalist methods which go with it. One of these is the individual ownership of land. To us in Africa, land was always recognised as belonging to the community. Each individual within our society had a right to the use of land, because otherwise he could not earn his living, and one cannot have the right to life without also having the right to some means of maintaining life. But the African's right to land was simply the right to use it; he had no other right to it, nor did it occur to him to try and claim one.'[1]

President Nyerere rejects emphatically the exploitation of man by man which he sees as the most reprehensible aspect of the Western system of capitalism in the individual ownership of and speculation in land. He equally rejects the

Eastern European version of socialism which preaches that a happy socialist society can be built only on a philosophy of conflict between man and man, that is by introducing and exploiting the theory of class warfare into African society. He sees African socialism as an attitude of mind. He lays great emphasis on sharing or distribution of the wealth of society by all members of the society, and condemns acquisitiveness for the purpose of gaining 'power and prestige' as unsocialistic.

President Nyerere's ideas of socialism in 1962 have further been clarified in the February, 1967, Arusha Declaration of the Tanganyika African National Union party (TANU). This Declaration maps out the road of socialism which Tanzanian leaders want Tanzanians to tread in the building of a happy and fair society in that country.

The Arusha Declaration is viewed by some observers as an extreme type of socialism which will not succeed in other parts of Africa because it precludes participation in public life by the most able citizens, who by dint of their labour, skills or ability to save, have accumulated some wealth, however small that wealth may be. The Tanzanian leaders believe, however, that it is no use preaching one thing and doing just the opposite. They look at Tanzania's problems through their own experiences and preach that if exploitation of man by man must cease in the country then the African revolution which they preach must start at home. The Tanzanian leaders see the Arusha Declaration as the fire to spark off this type of revolution.

The Declaration must also be seen as Tanzanian leaders' reaction to the predatory practices of the dethroned political leaders of West Africa, particularly those of Ghana, Nigeria, the Upper Volta and Sierra Leone, who plundered their nationals shamelessly through the use of their political offices and power. It is possible too that President Nyerere and his colleagues have also been disturbed by recent economic trends in neighbouring Kenya, where it appears an élite type of capitalism is emerging. The ascetic inspiration of the

Arusha Declaration is a complete departure from this type of development. The Declaration is Tanzania's own version of the new doctrine of African socialism, a doctrine still in the formative stage, tailored to Tanzania's needs and circumstances. The preamble of the Declaration sums up the complexes and the nature of the problems which the political leaders of Tanzania face. It says in part:

> 'We have been oppressed a great deal, we have been exploited a great deal and we have been disregarded a great deal. It is our weakness that has led to our being oppressed, exploited and disregarded. We now intend to bring about a revolution which will ensure that we are never again victims of these things.'[2]

Tanzanian leaders have rejected exploitation of man by man which capitalism introduced into Africa. They have denounced not only foreign capitalists and exploiters, but also their own home-spun ones. They argue that if socialism means that a few Tanzanians are to be given opportunities to get rich quick while the majority remain poor, then that type of socialism must be rejected with the scorn which it richly deserves. The Arusha Declaration aptly deals with the problems of political representation and the wealth-accumulating proclivities of the political élite. It declares, among other things, that:

1. 'Every TANU and Government leader must be either a peasant or a worker, and should in no way be associated with the practices of capitalism or feudalism.
2. No TANU or Government leader should hold shares in any company.
3. No TANU or Government leader should hold directorships in any privately-owned enterprises.
4. No TANU or Government leader should own houses which he rents to others.
5. For the purposes of this resolution, the term "leader" should comprise the following:—Members of the TANU national executive committee; ministers, members of parliament, senior officials of organisations affiliated to

TANU, senior officials of para-State organisations (i.e. nationalised or nationally-owned enterprises), all those appointed or elected under any clause of the TANU constitution, councillors and civil servants in high and middle cadres.'[3]

In Tanzania's circumstances the categories of persons who cannot serve their nation in any leadership position by virtue of these resolutions must be quite extensive. These categories include all educated men and women who would like to play some part in public life, not necessarily because they seek to enrich themselves at the expense of their fellow citizens, but for the sheer love of service. Some of them cannot in clear conscience become public servants at the expense of now abandoning or liquidating what little wealth they have acquired throughout the years. It is no surprise then that the Arusha Declaration has drawn cries of anguish from a large number of incumbent parliamentarians.

The Government has answered a number of questions asked by these parliamentarians about the real meaning of the Declaration and their own political future.

Two aspects of human nature revealed by the type of question asked about the meaning of the Declaration by the parliamentarians are self-interest and acquisitiveness, traits which the Tanzanian concept of socialism unreservedly condemns. For instance, question No. 3 asks:

'If a man has taken the lump sum pension he received after 15 years' service in the British civil service, and has invested that money in a house which he lets out, is it just to ask him to sell that house?'

The Government pamphlet gives this most interesting answer:

'If the man in question has no intention of holding a leadership position, either in the party or in the Government, it would be unjust to ask him to sell his house. No one is asking, or will ever ask, that he should do this. If, on the other hand, he wants a leadership position in the party or the Government, it is definitely not unjust to ask him to behave like 99·9 per cent of the people whom he says he wants to lead or serve.

They feel themselves to be lucky if they have a house of their own to live in—at least in the urban areas. Real leadership demands understanding and identification; this cannot be achieved while the leader is in a position which enables exploitation. And although the man in this case originally earned his pension, he may be accused of using his reward for exploitative purposes.

'It is important to be clear about this. Even if the individual is in fact receiving no more than a fair interest on his money—that is, no more than the Bank or Government would give—there are two other factors to be considered.

'The first is that he, a leader, will be in a position where he controls the shelter of another individual, who probably is not a leader and who might consequently feel himself at a disadvantage in any negotiations. The second is that either his tenant, or other people, may fail to understand that the rent being charged is a fair one, so that they will believe him to be exploiting them even if he is not. A leader should not involuntarily get into such a position; it should be absolutely obvious that he is not in a position to exploit another human being.'[4]

It is clear from this reply that any person who wants to enter public or political life in Tanzania must first make up his mind whether he wants to use his position to help create an aristocracy of power (or 'pull') or genuinely to serve his people. The Declaration does not discourage investment in real estate or business. On the contrary, what the declaration outlaws is the fraud perpetrated by some politicians elsewhere in Africa who claim that they are in politics to serve their fellow-men while their practices, such as ostentatious living, greedy plunder of the public coffers and their misuse of power, tell quite a different story. The Tanzanian brand of socialism makes it entirely clear that it would not accommodate the pretence that leaders can serve their fellow citizens and at the same time practise exploitation.

The reply to question No. 10 specifically deals with this contradiction and the future of incumbents and potential incumbents of political and public office in these words:

'Which is the politician who went to the people at election time and asked them to elect him so that he could provide for his future? Which Area or Regional Commissioner or other TANU worker got his job by saying he wanted to improve his personal position and get security for his future?

'Whenever a person seeks political work, whether it is through election or by appointment, he says he wants the opportunity to serve the people, to guard their interests and to further their aspirations. What right has such a person, once he has the appointment he sought on this basis, to use his responsibility for his own betterment?'[5]

By any political standards, the Arusha Declaration is a very austere document which asks of the Tanzanian élite a great deal of sacrifice, provided they wish to serve the public as 'politicians'. It places great strain on the manpower resources of the country and will probably dilute the quality of persons who will in future seek participation in public life. Tanzania, it should be noted, is not particularly blessed with super-abundance of this type of person. Though English is not the only official language for the conduct of business in parliament, some knowledge of that language is needed to be able to cope efficiently with the complicated procedures and business, not only of government but also of commerce. To limit membership of public bodies such as parliament and para-state organisations to only peasants and workers and those who are not regarded as 'exploiters and capitalists' is to strain the limited resources of any African country, particularly Tanzania, almost to breaking point.

It is also debatable whether the ascetic ideals of the Arusha Declaration will serve as an incentive to any local potential investors who might wish, in view of the limited foreign inflow of capital, to create new productive opportunities in their own country in the private sector of the economy. Such genuine potential entrepreneurs stand in grave danger of being categorised as 'exploiters and capitalists'. Another aspect of such limitation on genuine local entrepreneurs' participation in public life, particularly parliament, is that parliament might be placed squarely under the control of citizens who do not regard themselves as 'exploiters' and who might be very willing to enact legislation to destroy the businesses of even genuine investors on the shaky grounds that such businessmen are exploiting fellow-Tanzanians. This danger might not arise, however, if every business were under public control.

So far, it is not clear whether that is the ultimate goal of Tanzanian socialism. President Nyerere lays great emphasis on the distributive aspect of Tanzanian socialism. What is not equally emphasised is the source of the wealth to be distributed. There appears to be a fundamental assumption that this wealth is naturally there, and that all that remains is that it should be equally or equitably shared by all members of the society. President Nyerere rejects capitalism in any form and insists that Tanzania's economy must be built on self-reliance. He says there 'can be no such thing as acquisitive socialism, for that would be another contradiction in terms. Socialism is essentially distributive. Its concern is to see that those who sow reap a fair share of what they sow.'[6]

President Nyerere's description of traditional African society in his *Ujamaa* speech holds for a society which has largely disappeared. Over 70 years of colonialism and nearly a decade of independence have radically changed not only the economic basis of the original African societies but also the attitudes of individual members of these societies towards acquisition of property, methods of productivity and the allegiances of individuals in the community. The citizen in the traditional society had insurance against unemployment, sickness and famine because he lived in a small community and contributed his fair share to the wealth of the community. Today, he lives in a far larger and more complex society with new problems which his forebears had never faced. The harsh economic and social facts of contemporary African life have taught the individual citizen that however much he loves his community, society or nation, he must do his best to acquire at least the bare necessities—food, shelter and clothing for himself—if he means to live.

These harsh facts of economic and social life tend to turn all men towards becoming acquisitive creatures, whether they live in capitalist or socialist societies or not.

However, it should honestly be conceded that the Tanzanian Government's reply to question No. 10, quoted above, constitutes an appropriate, even though extremely harsh, reaction towards the anti-social activities of political leaders in certain African countries, particularly Ghana, Nigeria, the Upper Volta and Sierra Leone, and partly Tanzania itself. The unredeeming greediness for wealth displayed by ex-President Kwame Nkrumah of Ghana, his ministers, party activists and some other public men and women; their misuse of political power to deprive their fellow-citizens of human dignity through the enactment of pernicious laws and their rapacious plunder of the public chest for their personal aggrandisement constitute enough justification for any extreme measures designed to curb the excessive acquisitive propensities of politicians elsewhere in Africa.

It is against this background that the Arusha Declaration must be assessed. Tanzania's own problems of poverty, huge size and multi-racial population also serve as limiting factors to the rapid growth of the economy and its fair distribution of the wealth of the country. The Arusha Declaration should be seen, therefore, as a logical instrument designed to prevent politicians from using their political power and position from further aggravating the country's problems, particularly the exploitation of the under-privileged members of the society.

3
African Socialism in Action—II

IF THE TANZANIAN version of African socialism is considered extreme, the Kenya type must be considered very moderate indeed, or even as capitalism, depending upon one's own interpretation of what socialism is, at least, in practice.

The basic philosophy of the Kenya Government towards the building of the type of Welfare State envisaged by all African leaders is contained in its Sessional Paper No. 10 of 1963–65. The Sessional Paper spells out the various steps the Government intend to take to achieve rapid economic development through increasing the national wealth, raising the standard of living, ensuring fair distribution of land, creation of jobs, providing more and better schools, hospitals, and arranging old-age retirement benefits and social security for all in Kenya.

While accepting the Tanzanian aspect of mutual social responsibility, the Sessional Paper rejects forcible nationalisation of industry, except where continued operation in the private sector constitutes a danger to the national interest. The Kenya Government's approach to the economic question is stated in these words in paragraph 4 of the Sessional Paper:

> 'The ultimate objectives of all societies are remarkably similar and have a universal character suggesting that present conflicts need not be enduring. These objectives typically include:
>
> (i) political equality
> (ii) social justice
> (iii) human dignity including freedom of conscience
> (iv) freedom from want, disease and exploitation
> (v) equal opportunities and

(vi) high and growing *per capita* incomes equitably distributed.

'Different societies attach different weight and priorities to these objectives, but it is largely in the political and economic means adopted for achieving these ends that societies differ. These differences in means are, however, of paramount importance because ultimate objectives are never fully attained. Every time one target is attained a new one becomes necessary. Indeed, we forever live in transition.'[1]

Sessional Paper No. 10 was published nearly eighteen months after the attainment of independence. It reflects the general consensus in Kenya at that time. It was published after the issues of African socialism and its reflection on the Government's economic and social policies had been publicly debated by all the organised, articulate sections of the people in various regions of the country—parliamentarians, trade unionists, party leaders, university lecturers and students, and by the European and Asian settlers who controlled, at that time, over 90 per cent of Kenya's economy.

The document rejects on the one hand the assumption that once industries established by foreigners and operated by them are nationalised all the economic woes of the country will be solved. It equally rejects the exploitative and backward belief of some European and Asian settlers that private property is sacred and should not be disturbed under any circumstances. As a child of compromise, the Sessional Paper satisfied neither the left-wing extremists who wanted nationalisation at any cost nor the right-wing reactionaries who wanted to maintain the economic *status quo* at any cost, even after independence.

Some months after the publication of the Sessional Paper, it became clear that many of the left-wingers in the ruling KANU party were dissatisfied with the moderation of the Kenya Government, particularly in its refusal to nationalise certain industries established by Asian settlers.

Grumbling was also heard among this group over the conduct of Kenya's foreign relations. The fact was that most

of the left-wingers were ardent admirers of ex-President
Kwame Nkrumah of Ghana, whose noisy attitudisation in
inter-African relations they described as 'dynamic and progressive'. They became peeved by claims of Nkrumah's propagandists everywhere that Nkrumah was the most progressive African leader.

To minimise Nkrumah's claims, some of these left-wingers
argued that President Jomo Kenyatta, whom most Africans
regard as the foremost freedom fighter, should occupy the
centre of the stage in the efforts being made by African
leaders towards forging continental unity. The way to
achieve this ambition, the left-wingers argued, was for President Kenyatta to play a more dynamic role in foreign affairs.
Most of these left-wingers were supporters of former Vice-
President Oginga Odinga, the most fervent advocate of the
Chinese brand of communism in the Kenya Cabinet.

In the absence of an opposition party to blame (the Kenya
African Democratic Union party had dissolved itself in November, 1965) for their disaffection, the dissident ginger
groups within the Kenya Parliament, popularly known as the
'Socialist and Progressive' groups, turned against their own
leaders, the Cabinet Ministers.

By February, 1966, bitter frustration, disillusionment and
open antagonism between these dissidents and the Government permeated the Kenya political atmosphere. On February 15, 1966, these bitter differences culminated in a
marathon seven-hour acrimonious debate in the House of
Representatives. The debate was ostensibly staged to express
confidence in President Kenyatta and his Government.

It became clear as the debate developed, however, that it
was staged as a trial of strength between the dissidents and
the moderates in the KANU party and the Kenyatta Government.

Although the Government won an overwhelming vote of
confidence, it turned out to be only a temporary truce. The
debate itself revealed, perhaps for the first time in the open,
the deep cleavages between the left-wingers and the moder-

ates, a cleavage which eventually culminated in a split in the one-party KANU Government and the formation of the Kenya People's Union under former Vice-President Oginga Odinga. This was followed by the 'Little General Election' of June, 1966, in which the underdog party, the Kenya People's Union, won an overall majority of the votes cast but returned fewer candidates than the ruling KANU party.

The most interesting aspect of this vote of confidence debate was that it was sparked off by an innocuous remark made by the Finance Minister, Mr James Gichuru, in Lagos over the Rhodesian unilateral declaration of independence. Mr Gichuru was asked on a television programme whether he thought Rhodesian Africans were ready for an immediate take-over of power from the rebel regime of Ian Smith. He replied, 'Well, it would be very stupid if we were to ask for immediate take-over. The Africans in Rhodesia are not as well organised as they are here in West Africa, or as they are in East Africa, if I might claim that much.'[2]

Mr Gichuru had been representing the Kenya Government at the emergency Commonwealth Prime Ministers' conference in Lagos, called by the late Sir Abubakar Tafawa Balewa, the Federal Prime Minister of Nigeria, to find a solution to the Rhodesian problem after certain African Governments had broken diplomatic relations with Britain over her inability to resolve the Ian Smith rebellion. At the end of this conference Mr Gichuru made his remarks in reply to a television reporter's question, and his words were quoted in an article published in the Nkrumah-financed magazine *Africa and the World*, and certain statements which Mr Gichuru claimed he never made were attributed to him. But what really fomented trouble was the suggestion in the article that 'progressive-minded people are entitled to know who are their friends and who are their enemies in Kenya'.

The article, headed 'Kenya: Is the price of Unity too High?' was quoted *in extenso* by Mr Tom Mboya, Minister for Economic Planning and Development, during this long debate. He laid stress on some portions to show that the dissidents were being directed by foreign elements and agitators who wanted to subvert the Government of Jomo Kenyatta. He cited one particularly offensive portion of the article which read:

'We have felt that the question of national unity has been paramount in Kenya. Most Kenyans have taken the same view. They have felt respect for Kenyatta's great nation-building efforts, but one is entitled to ask to what end is the unity being built. If Kenya is not to be brought into increasing disrepute, those in its Government and outside who hold progressive views must speak out at once. They must proclaim their own position clearly and uncompromisingly. The continent of Africa is in a condition of revolutionary crisis. How that crisis is resolved is of importance to the whole of mankind. Progressive-minded people are entitled to know who are their friends and who are their enemies in Kenya. The time has passed for sitting on the fence.'[3]

Mr Mboya, who was the chief Government spokesman in this debate, proved himself not only a great Parliamentarian but a fervent believer in the Government's policies as enunciated in the KANU manifesto, the Sessional Paper No. 10, and the various policy declarations made by President Kenyatta's Government since the country's independence, and proved too that the Government was being guided by the mandate it had received from the electorate.

Mr Mboya objected to interference in Kenya's affairs by outsiders, particularly the pretensions of those sitting in London seeking with 'cool impudence' to choose leaders for Kenyans. He asked sarcastically: 'We want to know if there are any back-seat drivers of the affairs of our country, trying to direct it from outside this country. We want to know whether the people of this country elected us, so that we can serve the wishes of some so-called progressive elements internationally. This country deserves to know whether we are going to sing to the tune of some people who have taken it upon themselves to determine what the image of Kenya is going to be, and we want to know whether in this House or even in the Government there is a Member who believes that Kenya's reputation and image are going to be determined by somebody in London, in Washington, in Peking or in Moscow. I would even go further and say that our membership of the Organization for African Unity, our relations with any African State, preclude the right of the Organization for African Unity, the right of any State, to determine the destiny of the people of this country.'[4]

The Gichuru statement was only the spark that ignited the fire. The real cause of the political conflagration was a catalogue of simmering discontent, the result of disillusionment and propaganda against the Government for the apparently slow progress towards meeting the rising expectations of the ordinary citizens of Kenya in the economic and social fields. This discontent was craftily exploited by certain elements who went so far as to coin the phrase *uhuru nan n'jaa*— freedom and hunger—instead of the popular phrase *uhuru na kazi*—freedom and work—which was the promise made to the people during the struggle for independence. The build-up of general discontent developed gradually. The first signs came through the utterances of the rank and file of KANU activists and trade union leaders in the large towns and urban areas and echoed by their spokesmen in the two Houses of Parliament. These complaints are easily classified under five main heads:

1. That Asian and European settlers still had a stranglehold over Kenya's economy even after independence;
2. That land reform was progressing too slowly;
3. That there was discrimination in job allocation along tribal lines;
4. That retail trade was still largely in the hands of Asian settlers, even in the rural areas—a situation which militated particularly against the African consumers who perpetually complained against the sharp practices of the Asian shop-keepers; and
5. That housing was largely controlled by Asian and

European settlers who discriminated openly against Africans, including even the highly-educated Africans with good jobs.

Vice-President Oginga Odinga, undoubtedly a champion of the underdog in Kenya politics, did his best to give voice to these resentments and complaints of the ordinary African in all parts of the country. He and his supporters wanted speedy changes, faster rates of 'socialising' the public amenities, land and property, particularly industries. Naturally, his socialistic views fell like manna on the ears of the have-nots. Discouraged by the allegedly slow progress of his Cabinet colleagues towards implementation of the promises made to the electorate in the KANU manifesto, angered by the Government's handling of delicate issues such as the resettlement of the White Highlands and disillusioned by the coldness of his Cabinet colleagues towards his friends and benefactors, the Chinese communists, the former Vice-President became more and more isolated from his colleagues and their policies.

Mr Odinga did not help himself politically when he openly proclaimed that 'communism is like food to me'.

In retrospect, it could be said that it was this single statement that destroyed any lingering doubts in the minds of some of his admirers, staunch Cabinet colleagues and some of the ordinary people, and alienated his large following in Kikuyu areas of Kenya. The Kikuyu is passionately attached to his land, and believes in private property. He will not easily give his support to any politician who openly advocates 'socialising' his land or seizing his private property and throwing it into the common pool.

What further alarmed some of the KANU leaders was Mr Odinga's establishment of the Patrice Lumumba Ideological Institute near Nairobi for the training of party cadres in socialism. The Ideological Institute, as it turned out, was nothing but a carbon copy of the Kwame Nkrumah Ideological Institute at Winneba in Ghana. It was a school for propagating ideologies alien to many native Kenyans.

It was in this political atmosphere that the great debate was staged to clear the air so that all Kenya politicians could make their choice and decide on which road of socialism they want to travel. The choice was between the road mapped out in Sessional Paper No. 10 and Mr Odinga's Chinese road to socialism. The Kenyans chose the former.

In the first week of May, 1966, President Jomo Kenyatta introduced Kenya's £325 million Revised Development plan, 1966–1970. He said among other things:

> 'This Plan which the Government has prepared will remain a dead document if the people do not participate in making it a living reality. The spirit of *Harambee* (Let's pull together) must pervade all our activities. Already it is making a notable contribution to our development, through self-help activities. What the Government cannot give them (the people), however, is the *Will* to move ahead. I must underline that in some areas the process of economic and social development is held back by the unwillingness of the people to accept new ways and the necessary discipline of planned and co-ordinated development. Needless to say, no real development will take place unless the people want it and are prepared to work for that development and accept the necessary changes.'[5]

It is the philosophy behind this Revised Development Plan, 1966–1970, which more than anything else at that time brought into the open the ideological differences between the Kenya People's Union and the KANU Cabinet. While the KPU wanted a more rigid centrally-planned economy and development plan under which the Central Government would have more or less absolute power to dictate what would be done and where it would be done, who should do what and how it should be done, the KANU planners gave a large measure of freedom to the private and public sectors of the economy to contribute their share to the overall development of the country.

Here, a word about the meaning of planning seems to me essential.

Today, the Governments of nearly all countries, including

even that of the United States of America, are committed to the philosophy of economic growth; that is to say, how to increase a country's wealth so that all citizens can have at least the bare necessities of life—food, clothing and shelter. One of the most popular means of promoting economic growth in the poor nations of the world is through economic planning and development. This is the reason why most of the developing countries have established Ministries of Economic Planning and Development.

The main task of such ministries is to find out how the limited resources of a country—its natural and human resources—and foreign aid funds can be used to advantage so that the rising expectations of the people can be met without too much discontent from any sector of the population.

In Kenya, this task is performed by the Ministry of Economic Planning and Development under Mr Tom Mboya. All other ministries, however, also play important roles in the economic planning and development of the country.

In most developing countries, four important considerations must be kept in mind when drawing up a development plan. These are the existing physical, social, financial and economic factors in the country.

Physical planning deals mostly with the use of land, transport, design and layout of projects in both urban and rural areas of the country.

Social planning is concerned with welfare and social services, cultural development, self-help and community development, change of traditional or ancient attitudes and the elimination of social evils.

Financial planning deals with the problems of sources of Central Government revenue, its annual disbursement, creation of further wealth for investment and the establishment of banking and credit facilities and other financial institutions as a prop for the whole economy.

Economic planning involves the organisation of the country's real and monetary resources into a co-ordinated development effort.

To produce an efficient or successful development plan, the planners must take into consideration all these aspects of planning, otherwise no plan can materialise, however grandiose it may sound on paper. To produce a feasible plan, the planners must have adequate information on the country's actual and potential resources.

The planners must also have an accurate understanding of the objectives which the Government wants to promote with these resources. At the same time the planners must be informed about the economic behaviour patterns of the people when extra money comes into their pockets. The planners must ask themselves: do the salary and wage earners spend their extra money on drink, on building, education, clothing or on purchase of luxury goods such as radiograms, or on new farms or in establishing new productive industries? All these attitudes must be investigated before an accurate assessment of any development plan can be made.

Experience has shown that it is the business of the Statistical Department of the Governments—where they do exist—to gather this information for the planners. For it is this information which helps the planners to fix attainable targets in normal circumstances, that is to say without taking into consideration the occurrence of major disasters such as war, mutiny or violent earthquakes or unpredictable economic and political disturbances during the life of the plan. No economic plan, however adequate, can be implemented without proper co-ordination of the activities of all Government departments and the co-operation of the people in a country. It is also of vital importance that the people should have full knowledge of the plan through intensive publicity in all media.

One interesting aspect of the Kenya Revised Development Plan, 1966–1970, is that, unlike those of some African countries, it is not strictly centrally-oriented. There is opportunity for planning at lower levels. The Kenya Government believes that effective planning needs not only co-ordination of the activities of the Ministries and Local Government but also the development by these agencies of Government of sound projects that will contribute to the total picture of development strategy. For this reason, there is provision for a great measure of decentralisation. To ensure that there is close co-operation between the economic Ministries and the Ministry of Economic Planning and Development, provision was made for planning in the various Ministries where high officials would be allowed to do their own planning.

Physical planning, for example, is being done by the Town Planning department in the Ministry of Lands and Settlement. The Revised Plan provided for enlargement of the department to handle planning in the provinces and districts. Regional teams were to be appointed to supplement the work of the headquarters staff in Nairobi. Such regional teams would be closely associated with Provincial Development Committees.

Social planning is the responsibility of the Department of Community Development of the Ministry of Housing and Social Services. At Central Government level, social planning would be done side by side with economic planning. Community Development Committees in the Provinces were constituted as sub-committees of Provincial Development Advisory Committees to ensure co-operation in this sphere of planning. Provincial Planning Officers have been appointed to ensure that development activities at the provincial, district and municipal levels are carefully planned, co-ordinated and implemented.

In addition to these Provincial Planning Officers, various committees established in the provinces ensure full participation and co-operation at every level of carrying out development projects. All the provincial, district and municipal administrations which mainly collected taxes and rates during the colonial era are expected, under the Revised Development Plan, to make economic and social development their principal task through development advisory committees of prominent citizens and political leaders at all levels.

So far as the private sector is concerned, the Revised

Development Plan ensures that this sector be fully informed of the Government's plans to secure wholehearted co-operation in the development of industry, commerce, finance and agriculture. This information would be provided by the Ministries and the official statements of the President of the Republic to the proprietors of private industry, including informal contacts between economic ministries and business, finance and farm organisations. Provision has also been made for the formation of organised committees of leading citizens in the various sectors of private enterprise to advise economic ministries on plans in the private sector and to explain Government policies to those in private development. An Investment Protection Act accords guarantees to approved private firms and the Industrial Protection Committee will continue to play its role in recommending the grant of subsidies, industrial assistance, tariffs, duty drawbacks and other facilities to private firms.

Even the University College of Nairobi has a role to play in the economic development of the country. The College's Institute of Development Studies is playing an important part in data analysis. The planned Faculty of Building Design and Development will be of special value to the Town Planning department in the physical planning activities of the Ministry.

On the East African level, the Kenya Government maintains links with Uganda and Tanzania through existing institutions such as the East African Common Services Organisation, the University of East Africa and the Economic Community for Eastern Africa. These links are helping Kenya to promote more effective trade, co-ordinate industrial location, tariff policies and running of other common services.

The Kenya Revised Development Plan is the work, mainly, of the Development Committee, responsible to the Cabinet. It meets under the chairmanship of the Minister for Economic Planning and Development, with the Minister of Finance as vice-chairman. Its membership includes all Ministers connected with economic development. Other Ministers are free to attend at any time. (See chart on opposite page.)

The task of the Development Committee is to:

(a) review development plans for the public and private sectors of the economy;
(b) consider new proposals in relation to works and administrative capacity; available skilled manpower, sources of funds and social benefits and costs;
(c) assign priorities among proposed projects—to see that the country's limited resources are used constructively;
(d) recommend modifications or approved plans; and
(e) recommend modifications or changes in plans and methods for carrying out plans.

The Ministry, established on December 12, 1964, the first anniversary of Kenya's independence, took over the Directorate of Planning in the Ministry of Finance and Economic Planning. Today, it works through three principal units, namely: Administrative, Statistical and Planning Division.

The principal functions of the Administrative division are to manage technical assistance; to work in liaison with Parliament and the public; to co-ordinate international economic matters and to maintain close co-operation with the Ministries of Finance and Foreign Affairs, and the President's office. It keeps in close touch with the Ministry of Finance since the development plan cannot succeed without funds.

On the other hand, finance from outside the country depends largely on having a sound plan for orderly and peaceful development.

Further, since the supply of domestic finance for development is limited, a realistic plan cannot be produced without advance planning of the tax structure and knowledge of recurrent expenditure. It is the Finance Ministry that plays a vital role in these fields.

The Statistical division collects, correlates, analyses and publishes all statistical data gathered by the Government. It has already collected enough data on various aspects of the

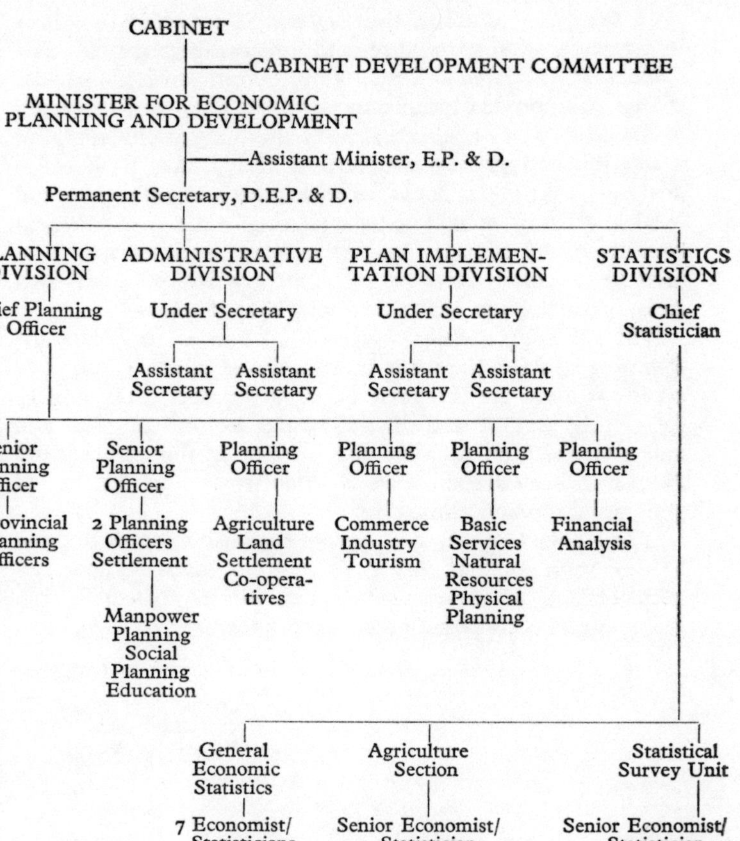
CABINET
CABINET DEVELOPMENT COMMITTEE
MINISTER FOR ECONOMIC PLANNING AND DEVELOPMENT
Assistant Minister, E.P. & D.
Permanent Secretary, D.E.P. & D.
PLANNING DIVISION
ADMINISTRATIVE DIVISION
PLAN IMPLEMENTATION DIVISION
STATISTICS DIVISION
Chief Planning Officer
Under Secretary
Under Secretary
Chief Statistician
Assistant Secretary
Assistant Secretary
Assistant Secretary
Assistant Secretary
Senior Planning Officer
Senior Planning Officer
Planning Officer
Planning Officer
Planning Officer
Planning Officer
Provincial Planning Officers
2 Planning Officers Settlement
Agriculture Land Settlement Co-operatives
Commerce Industry Tourism
Basic Services Natural Resources Physical Planning
Financial Analysis
Manpower Planning Social Planning Education
General Economic Statistics
Agriculture Section
Statistical Survey Unit
7 Economist/ Statisticians
Senior Economist/ Statistician
3 Economist/ Statisticians
Senior Economist/ Statistician
2 Economist/ Statisticians

country's economy, especially on the structure and activities of large-scale enterprises, agriculture, commerce and industry.

In the years to come, this division is expected to collect information on expenditure and savings patterns of consumers and business firms, input-output analysis of the economy, improved balance of payments data, and inventory of the economy's resources, sizes of and fluctuations in stocks, marketing and pricing structure in agriculture. It will also analyse Government activities with regard to municipal and local governments; collect data on small-scale enterprises in commerce and industry and agriculture; evaluate new projects in economic development, build up data on social attitudes, customs and aspirations and vital statistics.

The Planning division advises the Minister for Economic Planning and Development and the Development Committee on the strategy for economic development and is responsible for setting sectoral and district targets in both physical and value terms. The division also sees to it that the various Ministries keep to the targets set and that they are distributed geographically and equitably.

The Kenya Government plans to establish a fourth division to deal with implementation of projects, since without implementation no development plan, however feasible, can make any real contribution to development.

4
Strategy of Economic Development

IN THE LAST two chapters we discussed the application of the new doctrine of African socialism to the solution of economic problems in two East African countries, Tanzania and Kenya. We concluded that while Tanzania condemns the Western system of capitalism, particularly private ownership of land and exploitation of man by man through unequal economic opportunities, the Kenya Government accepts private ownership of land and private enterprise, as well as public ownership of sources of production of wealth as the best system for tackling that country's economic and development problems. We described at some length Kenya's Revised Development Plan, 1966–70, and emphasised the large measure of devolution of authority to regional planning bodies.

In this chapter, we shall examine the strategy of economic development in these new States and find out what obstacles these new States encounter in the implementation of their national economic development plans.

Every economic development plan is in reality just a dream. To make such dreams come true, human beings must wake up and translate their pleasant dreams into action. Every national economic development plan demands that the people of the country must play a part in making the plan a success, so that it may not remain only just a dream. One way of making such plans realities is to consider not only how much more could be produced, during the plan period, how much more money each citizen could earn, how much more foreign money or exchange could be earned to pay for capital goods, such as machinery, and how much high or low prices would fall, but also to ensure that all citizens play a part in the economic growth of the country.

No group of citizens, however enthusiastic they may be about their country's development plan, can play an effective role in its implementation if they remain largely a group without skills or exploitable talents in various fields. In like manner, the majority of citizens cannot play any effective part in the implementation of such plans if the wealth of the country is not fairly and equitably distributed.

The Governments of the developing States of Africa must ensure that in the exciting task of nation-building the ordinary citizens do not remain mere onlookers but are active participants in economic development. They can do this, first by improving the skills and experience of their people; second, by ensuring that the people play a greater part in managerial, technical and professional jobs; third, by giving the people more opportunities to own domestic sources of industry and agriculture for productive purposes, and lastly, by spreading economic development projects as evenly as possible throughout the whole territory.

These four goals or principles, if properly applied and co-ordinated, can ensure rapid social change. In other words, these four goals must be designed to change the pre-independence pattern under which many Africans owned very little or no sources of wealth or were merely labourers in the employ of European or immigrant races who controlled practically all sources of wealth in the former colonial territories.

Any determined African Government can change the socio-economic pattern through judicious application of sound economic principles in several ways; for example, through active participation or promotion in the production of wealth; by encouraging the establishment of co-operative societies in agriculture, wholesale and retail trade; by encouraging self-help schemes throughout its territory; by encouraging private industry and investors (where these are welcomed) to play their full part in the economy of the country; and by training and education of the population so that many more people can come into the money sector of the economy, thus leading to the equitable sharing of the wealth which they themselves have produced.

Each development plan or project generates ancillary or secondary services. But no development plan can take off successfully without certain pre-conditions. Some of these are:

(a) a fairly large educated population;
(b) trained administrators and technicians at all levels;
(c) efficient means of transportation, communications, abundant supply of power;
(d) fairly accurate listing of priorities—that is to say, which projects should be executed first and which later, and
(e) a dynamic, ambitious population, willing, able and ready to play their part in 'lifting themselves up by their bootstraps'.

These factors have been called the 'sinews of industrialisation' by some eminent economists. Whatever the name, it is largely true that no dynamic or sustained economic development can take place in any developing country without some or most of these sinews or factors of industrialisation.

It is for each national Government to decide where to lay emphasis in the implementation of its development plan, provided these sinews of industrialisation exist. Where they do not exist, or exist in an uneven proportion, it is for the Government to provide them before setting forth on any ambitious development programme. The provision of these sinews of industrialisation is tantamount to laying a sound foundation for future execution of development projects.

In the example of the Kenya Revised Development Plan already mentioned, great emphasis has been placed on education as the key which will open the door to further advancement. However, the plan also emphasises the development of agriculture and in particular the expansion of output, productivity and employment on small farms. It is the Government's view that there need be no conflict between industrialisation and improvement in agriculture because in Kenya's circumstances, the two, industry and agriculture, are complementary.

The Kenya Government has two sets of priorities in agricultural development, one for over-populated areas and one for the under-populated areas of the country. In the over-populated areas the priorities are:

(i) changing the means of production and the transport and distribution of new farm products;

(ii) provision of markets and transport facilities for increased farm products; and

(iii) the provision of markets, transport and communications so as to diversify consumption and savings out of the increased incomes of the farm population in particular and the public in general.

In the under-populated areas the priorities are as follows:

(a) provision of market, transport and communications to supply consumption and saving outlets for incomes, if and when earned;

(b) the provision of markets and transportation for the sale of increased farm crops to be produced with more effort, even with existing antiquated methods of farming; and

(c) changing the methods of production and the provision of markets to supply the new products of the farmers.

It is obvious that all these changes need a readjustment of the relationship between industry and agriculture, and that is why so much emphasis is placed on the modernisation of the latter, an industry on which most of the people depend for their livelihood during the plan period.

It is hoped that the expansion of agriculture, the setting up of national farms, the establishment of shopping centres in the urban and rural areas by the Government, the expansion of retail trade for the benefit of African traders through Government help and the establishment of new industries, such as the pulp paper mill planned for Broderick Falls, will all generate demand for new services.

These services will include demand for more rail space, airports, better roads, posts and telecommunications, more electricity, more police protection, and better information. These services will have to be provided along with the expanding agriculture and industrial establishments.

These services will in their turn generate more construction, thus providing jobs for the building trades—masons, carpenters, plumbers, electricians, fitters and handymen of all categories. Both Government agencies and private industry will have their part to play in these endeavours.

In West Africa, Ghana's abandoned First Seven-Year Development Plan, 1963–1970, is perhaps the prototype of African socialism carried to the extreme to achieve an economic goal, namely the 'socialisation' of all sources of productivity in an African country. The basic philosophy is stated in the Plan itself, and according to this document ex-President Nkrumah intended to 'socialise' the whole economy of Ghana in twenty years.

The Ghanaian type of African Socialism is clearly described in the following extract from the First Seven-Year Development Plan:

'Ghana has chosen the socialist form of society as the objective of her social and economic development. This choice is based on the belief that only a socialist form of society can assure Ghana a rapid rate of economic progress without destroying the social justice, that freedom and equality, which are a central feature of our traditional way of life.

'Our socialist policy is based on certain fundamentals, which include the following:

(i) The economy must be developed rapidly and efficiently so that it shall, within the shortest time possible, assure a high rate of productivity and a high standard of living for each citizen based on gainful employment.

(ii) The income from our physical assets and from the labour of our people applied to these assets year by year must be utilised for socially purposeful ends. Never must public want and private affluence be allowed to coexist in Ghana. And among the most important ends that the community must provide for out of its incomes should be the education and welfare of its children, and the continued expansion of the economy itself.

(iii) The community through its government must play a major role in the economy, thus enabling it to assure the maintenance of a high level of economic activity, the provision of adequate employment opportunities, the equitable distribution of the nation's output, and the availability of the means of satisfying over-riding social ends.

'The building of a socialist society is not an easy task. In other countries the progress toward socialism has not been smooth or rapid—even the pioneers in this enterprise are still in the process of building socialism. The path that Ghana chooses toward socialism must be one that will lead us at the end to a prosperous and just society.'[1]

Under this plan, the Government recognised five sectors in the Ghanaian economy, all operating side by side. These sectors are:

1. State enterprises;
2. Enterprises owned by foreign private interests;
3. Enterprises jointly owned by the State and foreign private enterprise;
4. Co-operatives; and
5. Small-scale Ghanaian private enterprise.

According to Nkrumah, State enterprises are those enterprises completely owned and operated by the State, including all enterprises managed under the direction of governmental organs. The main aims of operating State enterprises, according to Nkrumah, are:

'Firstly, to ensure an ever-growing and steady employment for the people.

'Secondly, to increase national income and the revenues of

the state in order to raise the living standards of the people, to expand and improve both education and health services.

'Thirdly, to have at the command of the state significant and growing stocks of commodities in order to be able to influence the market, this influence being aimed at the stabilisation of the price level and that of currency.

'Lastly, to supply those services which the private sector does not wish or is not allowed to supply.'[2]

Every Government has to decide in which sector of the economy to invest money, which to emphasise and which to leave to the private sector. The Ghana experience shows that it is sometimes dangerous for the State to put all its resources into one basket, in this case, the industrial one. Nkrumah established no fewer than 53 State enterprises by February 23, 1966. The Auditor-General's report on these enterprises showed clearly that they constituted a great drain on the slender resources of the country, and in most cases the only reason for their establishment was to provide 'jobs for the boys'. But Nkrumah did not hide this motive from the people. It was his own stated first reason, namely, 'to provide employment for the people'.

After his dismissal from office, his own Economic Consultant, Mr Ayeh Kumi, revealed that even in the fifth sector, where small-scale Ghanaian private entrepreneurs were allowed to operate, Nkrumah did everything to destroy their business. The stated aim was to kill private initiative so as to prevent the emergence of a dynamic middle-class population wealthy enough to challenge his political leadership.

Foreign private enterprise also did not fare well under the Nkrumah brand of African socialism, despite his protestations to the contrary. The difficulties encountered through export licensing, the artificial shortage of raw materials to feed the factories and the rapacious plunder of these foreign private firms by the Nkrumah-inspired bribe-collecting agency, NADECO (National Development Company) all but killed any meaningful industrialisation in the country by February 24, 1966.

Though Nkrumah's practice of African socialism differed greatly from his theories, he always sought to blame others for his failure to attract more foreign investors into the country in his final years as President of Ghana. In a speech to a group of foreign businessmen at Flagstaff House in Accra on February 22 1963, Nkrumah had this to say about private investment in Ghana:

> 'Our ideas of socialism can coexist with private enterprises. I also believe that private capital, and private investment capital in particular, has a recognised and legitimate part to play in Ghana's economic development. We are consistent in these ideas. I have never made any secret of my faith in socialist principles, but I have always tried to make it quite clear that Ghana's socialism is not incompatible with the existence and growth of a vigorous private sector in the economy.
>
> 'Gentlemen, I need hardly say that Ghana expects you—indeed, Ghana invites you—businessmen, industrialists, bankers, manufacturers, and investors—to play a significant role in this economic growth and development. . . . Those of you who will be investing in Ghana will be investing in a very stable country; a country united; a country determined to make progress; a country determined to industrialise; a country determined to mechanise and diversify its agriculture; a country dynamic and honest in its intentions and consistent in its policies.
>
> 'Look around the country for yourselves. Invite your business friends to come here and see with their own eyes the happy atmosphere pervading everything we do; the stability we rightly boast of; the buoyancy of our economy and the happy relationships existing between all races who live here. There can be no better assurance to investors than these.
>
> Tell them not to be taken in by the mischief of a section of the press in Europe and America.'[3]

The shocking revelations made before the various commissions of enquiry established by the National Liberation Council after the February 24, 1966 *coup d'état* showed clearly that the economy of Ghana collapsed not because of the 'mischief of a section of the press in Europe and America', but because of the criminal and reckless dissipation of the natural and human resources of the country by the Convention People's Party rule of Kwame Nkrumah and that regime's unsuccessful attempt to force down the throats of unwilling Ghanaians their false ideology of 'scientific socialism', an ideology completely alien to the Ghanaian way of life.

Nkrumah's 'scientific socialism' collapsed because he and his 'gaping sycophants' of the one-party State forgot that Ghanaians have 'a deep-rooted reverence for land as the foundation of community life'. The Constitutional Commissioners explained this phenomenon in paragraph 696 of their draft constitutional proposals in these words:

> 'This remark—a deep-rooted reverence for land as the foundation of community life—springs from the fact that land has played a very important part in the political and economic history and development of this country. What is regarded as the first organised protest on a national scale started with the creation of the Aborigines Rights Protection Society in 1897. The formation of this Society was the culminating point in a series of agitations against the British Government in respect of its attitude towards land in this country.'[4]

The Nkrumah brand of African socialism died a premature death in Ghana because, according to the draft constitutional proposals, 'we in Ghana have known from time immemorial the concept of property held in trust for the benefit of a number of people. Stool property and land generally have for ages been held by Stools for the benefit of the community as a whole.'[5]

Under the guise of 'scientific socialism' the leaders of the CPP feverishly seized large tracts of land for the establishment of State Farms without, in some cases, paying compensation to the owners of these plots of land. There were cases where land had been acquired ostensibly in the public interest but really for a particular individual. 'The principle that in order to constitute public use it is essential that an entire community should directly participate in or enjoy an improvement in a particular land or property which is taken for the public use was thrown to the winds.'[6]

The journalist, Colin Legum of the *Observer* newspaper of London, identifies two factors that militate against the socialist system in Ghana. He writes:

'A brief examination of Ghanaian society elucidates the background in which the present political patterns have developed. Ghana's society is characterised by strong individualism operating within ethnocentric communal patterns. This makes for strong tribal and regional interests and for individual enterprise, two factors that militate against socialist ideas. This reaction has been strongest among the peasants, the fishermen, the traders, and the middle class. Although land is mostly communally owned through the traditional system of tribal stool lands, practice allows for individual possession during the lifetime of the occupant, and usually for his descendants. Thus the vital cocoa crop is raised by individual peasant producers. The pattern of co-operative marketing—introduced by the colonial government—was only reluctantly accepted by the cocoa farmers after its practical advantages became apparent. But they resist any idea of collectivisation of cocoa production.

'Trading patterns are also strongly developed in Ghanaian society. The "market mammies"—a significant force in bringing the CPP to power—vigorously insist on their right to individual trading; every attempt to limit their opportunities has met with strenuous opposition. Independence opened up opportunities for Ghanaians to develop large-scale business and manufacturing enterprises, which were quickly seized by a small but powerful group of traders, mostly supporters of the CPP.

'Modern socialism has no popular roots in Ghanaian society. Its present influence is not primarily a response to needs felt by the masses of workers and peasants; it is the result of a deliberate choice of policy by Nkrumah and an élite in the CPP. They see socialism as the best method of meeting the needs of developing African society and of overcoming the problems of colonialism. The task of this élite group has been to popularise the idea of socialism and to win the country over to its acceptance; but they have not hesitated, on occasion, to adopt socialist measures against popular opposition.'[7]

It became obvious to Ghanaians that the Nkrumah type of 'scientific socialism' was nothing but blatant, impudent plunder of the citizens by, and to enrich, the élite gang of 'gaping sycophants' of the party and the party leader and life chairman, Dr Kwame Nkrumah. Having seen through this system of scientific socialism for what it was—a complete fraud, a socialist system more rapacious than all the predatory exploits of the notorious robber barons of the nineteenth century United States—most of the more unscrupulous party rank and file joined in the act. Thus were the state enterprises plundered, their property stolen with impunity and thousands of unproductive workers engaged to share in the loot of public coffers and wild dissipation of public property. No wonder few of these state enterprises made any profits at all!

The transitional regime of the National Liberation Council has not abandoned the five-sector management of Ghana's economy outlined in the First Seven-Year Development Plan. What is being done is to salvage as much as possible out of the wreckage. For this reason, a new organisation, the Ghana Industrial Holding Corporation, was established in September, 1967, to take over all the assets, rights, liabilities and obligations of the State Enterprises Secretariat which had hitherto managed the State enterprises. This new company is expected to operate the state enterprises which have not yet been sold to private investors and turn them into profitable and efficient concerns. The principle of 'jobs for the boys' will have to be discarded if this new company is to succeed.

African socialism means many things to many people. It ranges from the admixture of the free-wheeling and partially planned economies of such countries as Nigeria, Senegal and

Kenya to the rigidly planned economies of Tanzania, Ghana, Guinea and Mali. Nearly every African Head of State, with the possible exceptions of Presidents William V. S. Tubman of Liberia, the late Leon Mba of Gabon and Emperor Haile Selassie of Ethiopia, have at one time or another paid lip-service to the concept of African socialism in discussions pertaining to economic development and programming.

The one country in West Africa where this concept of African socialism has yet to be applied in development programming is Liberia, the oldest republic on the continent. Economically, Liberia is firmly wedded to the principles of free trade and private enterprise. No foreign exchange or trade controls have ever been imposed on the economy of the country; identical duties are levied on imports from all countries and there are no preferential tariffs. The country itself is blessed with an abundance of natural resources. Liberia's chief exports are iron ore, rubber, rough diamonds, coffee, cocoa, palm kernels, cola nuts and some piassava fibre.

The quality of Liberia's iron ore deposits is regarded as among the highest in the world. During the last twenty years Liberia's foreign trade increased nearly seventeen times. In 1945, foreign trade earnings amounted to just 15 million dollars. In 1965, the country recorded foreign trade earnings of 250 million United States dollars. During the same period, Government revenue rose from 2 million dollars to some 50 million dollars. Over the years, Liberia has consistently maintained a favourable foreign trade balance. In 1966, her external trading surplus was 37 million dollars and the figures might even be better for 1967 and 1968. As Africa's leading exporter of high grade iron ore, Liberia has benefited from improved world market prices.

President Tubman's 'open door' policy for foreign businessmen has been the key to the country's remarkable economic growth—as high as five per cent per annum, one of the highest in Africa. This policy has led to the dominance of the economy by foreign business concerns, the most important ones being the giant Lamco iron ore syndicate and the

Firestone rubber concessions. Many observers have criticised the agreements governing these concessions, particularly that of Lamco, and asked whether the profit-sharing arrangement between the Liberian Government and Lamco was really to the advantage of Liberia. These criticisms are based on the fact that apart from a very small rent for the concession Lamco pays no tax. The Government, however, gets about half the distributed profits: $37\frac{1}{2}$ per cent as dividend on its own stock and $12\frac{1}{2}$ per cent as tax on the share of profits due to Bethlehem Steel of the United States.

With such favourable concession agreements, the high prices for mineral exports, the relatively small population and the abundance of natural resources, it is easy to jump to the conclusion that Liberia must be one of the richest countries in West Africa, where development is evenly spread throughout every region of the country. The reality is otherwise.

Liberia's dilemma is the apparent impossibility of translating into a higher standard of living for the country as a whole the spectacular growth in the value of exports from these foreign concessions.

There are various reasons for this inability to spread development all over the country. The fact is that while the foreign concerns dispose of vast capital and great expertise the Central Government machinery is weak compared to those of former colonies, particularly the Anglophone ones.

In these former British colonies there exists a professional civil service whose officers are competent enough, who by long-established convention are not allowed to indulge in operating private businesses while still public officers. For these reasons they devote all their energies to running the business of the public. In Liberia, there is hardly a well-defined line of demarcation between civil servants and private businessmen. The real obstacle to real economic development in Liberia, therefore, is social not financial. The authors of a book, *Growth Without Development*, describe vividly the Liberian problem in these words:

'Liberia's most pressing need at the present time is not for more public buildings, roads, hospitals or schools, but rather for improved practices and organisational arrangements to enhance social participation in economic development, without which the social capital is incapable of inducing structural change.'[8]

Pursuing the argument further, the authors add:

'Liberia is fortunate in having a rich resources base relative to population. With an intelligent and honest development policy, the material and cultural lives of all Liberians could be markedly improved within a generation. What is needed initially is a simple programme, concentrating on increased production of rice and fish, the transformation of subsistence agriculture, improved education and vocational training, and the creation of a new line of domestic manufacture and processing . . . But our policy prescriptions for economic development are a waste of effort if the governing authorities have no intention of developing the national economy and all the Liberian people.'[9]

In other words, Liberia is registering economic growth but this growth is benefiting only a small section of the Liberian people. The growth is also retarded by uneven distribution of the 'sinews of industrialisation'.

The authors of *Growth Without Development* have their own prescription for correcting this state of affairs in Liberia. They insist that the primary obstacle to economic progress in Liberia is social and not financial in these words:

'The primary obstacles to economic progress in Liberia are not technical but social-political and institutional residues of an earlier era . . . Liberia is being run—and run inefficiently in terms of development—by a handful of people. Close family ties developed in response to earlier pioneer conditions inhibit efficient conduct of government by encouraging nepotism and large-scale outlays for unproductive purposes.'[10]

One way to spread development evenly, not only in Liberia but in other African countries with similar economic patterns, is to put an end to educational policies which have held back indigenous tribes from a full share in the development of all sectors of their national economy.

The United Nations proclaimed the decade 1960–70 as the 'development decade'. It was expected that during these years the rich nations, mostly the industrialised Western nations, Japan and the Soviet Union, would allocate about one per centum of their Gross National Product to the development of the poor or developing nations.

In 1965, half-way through the 'development decade', a conference was held at Cambridge University, England, on economic development to discuss the progress achieved so far. The conference, sponsored by the British Ministry of Overseas Development, was attended by representatives of African Governments, international agencies, businesses and universities, as well as delegates and observers from Asia, Latin America, the Middle East and the Caribbean. The conference discovered that there have been several disappointments during the decade of development, among them three of particular significance to the new nations of Africa, namely:

(i) the rate of increase in national incomes has in general been slower than during the 1950s;
(ii) the net rate of increase in foreign funds becoming available for development is levelling off; and
(iii) the whole concept of 'economic take-off' is now regarded as unrealistic, and that it is much more difficult to sustain development than to initiate it—as the state enterprises in Ghana have so convincingly demonstrated.

The most important conclusion of the Cambridge conference is that the next half of the development decade may see a backward trend in development programming because the foreign funds on which most new states of Africa depend are drying up.

5
Economic Aid as Ideological Weapon

THE DRAMATIC differences between the rising expectations of the people of the independent states of Africa and the appalling economic and social conditions that 'begin where the pavement ends' will continue to plague the continent for a long time yet. It is the agonising appreciation of these differences that led the leaders of the new states to set their development targets far above what they can achieve by exploiting their own meagre natural and human resources. It is the same reason that has compelled them to rely on foreign aid, handouts, loans, bilateral, multilateral and international economic agreements of various kinds to carry through much needed development projects. And while these differences exist, 'neo-colonialism' and 'neo-imperialism' will continue to plague African politics because most of these new states cannot exist, let alone achieve any significant and meaningful development, without investment and technical aid from abroad and foreign markets for their products. It is this never-ending search for massive financial and technical aid from overseas that has introduced the Cold War between the Western and the Sino-Soviet bloc of states into African politics and economic relations.

Until 1956, the Western bloc provided the major foreign aid funds for carrying out development projects in the colonies—and the newly independent states of Asia, Africa and Latin America. The reasons are partly historical and partly deliberate. Even by 1967, Communist bloc economic assistance and technical aid had reduced only slightly the Western European and United States position as the principal sources of help in developing African nations. How did this come about?

The idea of extending economic aid to the developing nations became fashionable in Western Europe after the success of George Marshall's great idea, the Marshall Plan. When the former United States Secretary of State, General George Catlett Marshall, mooted his great economic recovery programme of United States financial aid to certain European countries in June, 1947, to rejuvenate their wartorn economies many doubting Thomases booed the idea. They did not think it would succeed.

But the success of the Marshall aid programme to Western Europe persuaded the Western European countries themselves that the experiment could be successful if applied in some of the backward colonies over which they still held suzerainty. The rationale was that the better the living standards of these colonials the more their own manufactured goods would sell in the colonial markets. Western European aid is motivated, therefore, not only by moral considerations but equally by hard economic factors.

Economic aid means many things to many people. The United Nations describes it as 'outright grants plus net long-term lending for non-military purposes by governments and international organisations'. Experience has shown, however, that what both donor and recipient nations regard as economic aid covers many fields, including the military. Whatever the form of aid—whether outright grants, loans, gifts or technical and cultural—the fact is that both Western and the Sino-Soviet bloc of nations have poured large sums of money into Asia, Africa and Latin America since the end of World War II.

This economic aid has been, and is still being, given on government-to-government basis and/or through private investment in the economies of the developing nations.

As far back as 1929, the British Government, for instance, had enacted a Colonial Development Act, which was further extended in a 1940 Colonial Development and Welfare Act to help economic development in the colonies. By 1945, the amount the United Kingdom was prepared to spend on these development and welfare schemes had doubled. Similarly, in 1935, the French had instituted a development fund to provide investment resources for their colonies. This initial French plan was followed by a ten-year development plan after World War II. Belgium, the Netherlands, the Federal Republic of Germany and Italy became donor countries after the ratification of the Treaty of Rome, establishing the European Economic Community or the Common Market of which they are signatories. The Scandinavian countries and Canada became donor countries in the early 1960s.

These bilateral efforts at economic assistance to the developing nations of Africa are supplemented by international aid schemes through the Specialised Agencies of the United Nations, the International Monetary Fund, the International Finance Corporation, the *Organisation for Economic Co-operation and Development* (OECD) and The United States Agency for International Development (AID).

Each of the donor countries extends economic, technical and even cultural aid to the developing countries under specially agreed terms. It is in this sphere—the terms of agreement—that the ideological warfare between the two blocs intrudes itself into the politics of Africa.

For example, the Federal Republic of Germany extends economic aid to the developing countries on what the current Minister of Economics, Professor Karl Schiller, describes as a 'politico-economic basis', and not on political myths. This has not always been so. In 1964, the Secretary of State for the West German Ministry for Development Aid, Dr Vialon, coined the famous slogan *'Kein Geld für Feinder'* (No money for enemies), as the basis for extending West German aid to the developing countries. According to this philosophy, the West German Ministry for Development saw no reason why aid should be extended to the 'enemies' of the Federal Republic.

In course of time two main considerations emerged as

those governing the application of West German aid and investment in the new states of Africa. The first is political: the need to conduct an impressive public relations campaign for West Germany's claim to be the only legitimate German state and to dam the influence of East German development programmes in whatever territory it may be found. The second consideration of West German application of economic aid is to encourage the growth of private industry, rather than state enterprises, in the countries to which aid is extended. As a country that had prospered through private enterprise for centuries, the West Germans naturally extol the virtues of private enterprise. Former Chancellor Dr Ludwig Erhard, during his tenure of office, specifically laid down the aim of Federal aid as 'the creation of a stable middle class in the developing nations of Africa'. But a more cogent reason for the emphasis on private enterprise is the tight budget of the Federal Government in Bonn, which limits the amount of direct governmental aid that West Germany can extend to these new states.

The application of the Hallstein Doctrine, which forbids West German aid to countries that extend diplomatic recognition to the East German Government, had strained relations between West Germany and several African countries, particularly the Republic of Tanzania, and held up a number of aid schemes promised by the Federal Government. The modification or less strict application of the Hallstein Doctrine during the last two years has to some extent changed the West German attitude towards extension of development aid to the new countries. West Germany's bilateral aid, as compared with its multilateral aid, is in the ratio of five to one as against the average ratio of nine to one in the rest of Western Europe. This is so because West Germany entered the field in the late 1950s.

By 1964, the West Germans established six institutions for extending aid to the new African states. These are:

(i) *The German Development Corporation,* a private company, sponsored by the Federal Government, which owns most of its shares and put up 25 milliard of the 75 milliard marks capital. Established in 1962, the German Development Corporation sponsors and helps German industry by investing in locally formed companies by buying shares. Once the company becomes stable, these shares are sold and the money thus retrieved is re-invested in another project on a revolving basis.

(ii) *The German Foundation for Developing Countries (Deutsche Stiftung)*, established in 1959, organises personal contacts and supplies information for West Germans concerned with development problems. By 1964 this Foundation had conducted 65 meetings and 44 expert discussions for West German development concerns. At the same time it had held 46 international seminars for 1,160 leaders from 82 developing nations at which problems ranging from agriculture to technical training for the nationals of the developing countries were discussed.

(iii) *The German Development Service*, an equivalent of the American Peace Corps, concentrates on supply of young German workers and skilled technicians for the developing countries. In the summer of 1964, for instance, 44 young men and women went to Tanzania to work on housing projects. Since then many more have served in almost every African country.

(iv) *The German Institute for Development Policy*, which was established in Berlin in March 1964, trains university graduates for work in international aid agencies.

(v) The states of the Federal German Republic, the *Lander*, conduct their own development programmes; and

(vi) The West German Churches have their own offices for development aid. The Evangelical Church, for instance, which has had long association with some of the Churches in Africa, had by 1964 received 32m. marks from the Federal Government for 45 separate projects in the developing countries of Africa.

West German private investment in the new states of Africa plays a second role to that of public money, even though there are some limiting factors such as the absence of an existing commercial base to build upon, lack of experience and the keen competition from French and British contractors. Despite these disadvantages, private West German capital has played and will continue to play a vital role in the private sector in the new states in the years to come.

One West German company which is playing a vital role in the private investment field in Africa is the Hamburg company FRUKOGOLD. This firm started an interesting experiment in industrialisation in Ghana nearly three years ago, combining the many advantages and eliminating some of the disadvantages of industrialisation in the new countries. This company constructed all at once a network of technologically and economically connected factories in an Interlocking Industrial Food Complex at Tema, Ghana's new harbour, 18 miles east of Accra. This Interlocking Industrial Food Complex, as its entrepreneur, Noe Drevici, calls it, processes locally produced as well as imported raw material.

The capacity of the complex is designed in a way that profits beyond break-even point are possible although cost and sales prices are calculated on the basis of world market prices and although the quality of the foods produced is in accordance with international standards. Furthermore, the capacity is sufficient to meet Ghana's own requirements in each product concerned.

The Interlocking Industrial Food Complex is built in such a way that all service departments, including administration, are centralised. An experimental bakery has been placed in the uppermost storey of the mill where the mixing of local raw material with baking can be tested and controlled. Extensive warehouses for finished goods as well as cooling, freezing and deep-freezing facilities are available.

The Tema Interlocking Industrial Food Complex project clearly demonstrates the multiple challenges and the abundant possibilities which the requirements and problems of the developing countries offer to the industry, technology and research, especially of the advanced industrial countries, in the supply of packaging and other machinery, development of moisture-proof or humidity-proof and insect-resisting packages, the solution of the various corroding problems in tropical climates. The unique aspect of the Drevici Complex, Tema, is that it was not created on purely ideological grounds, nor was it conceived as just another industrial investment to provide 'jobs for the boys'. It was conceived and built on a sound industrialisation policy which holds that such industrialisation can only be successful if it leads to the creation of better living conditions and if it provides the local population with cheaper and better goods and services which the individual wants and is actually able to purchase.

West German entrepreneurs as well as Federal Government leaders realise that they cannot withdraw to a splendid isolation because they know that the older industrialised and the developing nations are living in one world. In his speech at the second United Nations Conference on Trade and Development (UNCTAD) in New Delhi in February 1968, the West German Minister of Economics, Dr Karl Schiller, put the new attitude of the German people in these words:

'We cannot recognise a so-called natural law according to which the old industrialised nations always enjoy higher rates of their *per capita* incomes than do the developing countries. Progress indeed must become world-wide.'[1]

But in their efforts to bridge the gap between developing and the older industrialised nations the German Minister warned: 'Development is not only a technological but also, and very largely, a social problem, calling for sociological reforms. All help for developing countries will be in vain if the aid only preserves old social structures or if the course of development is dissipated in what might be called a kind of bazaar capitalism.'[2]

French aid to the new states of Africa is, for historical reasons, based on quite different ideas and relationships. France considered her colonies as a kind of extension of the metropolitan economy. She supplied most of the manufactured goods needed in the colonies and these colonies in turn supplied all the raw materials which France could not grow herself. At Independence in 1960, France gave generous aid to these former colonies on the same theory that the new states were appendages of the mother country. French policy-makers did not contemplate that one day a country like Guinea, for example, would sever all economic links with her and proclaim her independence in unmistakable terms. Thus at Independence France signed new economic and monetary agreements with all the major countries, with the exception of Guinea, which were members of the franc zone.

Under these treaties the new states were to consult with France on their annual import programmes. This meant that France would continue to buy her staple crops at preferential prices from the markets of the new states in return for what amounted to the African states' veto on imports of too many manufactured goods from sterling and dollar countries. Part of the bargain was that France agreed to provide unlimited foreign exchange for the new states so long as they remained in the franc zone. France also guaranteed the convertibility of the local francs, which most of these states use, into French francs, and placed no controls on the transfer of profits both ways. But the effect of this last arrangement is that most of the profits from commercial operations in the Francophone areas are repatriated to France, leaving the economies of the new states no better or only slightly better than they were before Independence, even though they obtain guaranteed and higher prices from France than prevailed on the open world market.

This was the French system of economic aid and trade relations with the new states of Africa before the signing of the Yaounde Convention which made eighteen African states associates of the European Economic Community.

Under the Yaounde Convention, other members of the Economic Community were to be progressively allowed into the African market on the same terms as France. It is too early to say whether the degree of French control over the economies of the franc zone countries would be substantially reduced as a result of the Yaounde Convention.

When the Yaounde Agreement was signed in July, 1964, it was expected that the benefits that would accrue to the eighteen associated members would be so great that the Anglophone states would find themselves at great disadvantage. Events have demonstrated since then that the benefits of association have not been as great in some respects as was hoped by the associates. The economies of some states have been disturbed by changes in the system of support for commodity exports, from a bilateral one with France to a virtually free market system based on world prices. Senegal's groundnuts industry is the typical example of such a case. Because of this type of unforeseen change, the European Economic Community has assumed a greater role in the field of economic aid-giving in the associated states.

One institution which the EEC uses to extend aid to the new states in Africa is the European Development Fund. This institution has earmarked not less than 800 million United States dollars to be spent on aid programmes between 1964 and 1969 in the associated countries in Africa.

Two development funds, each to run for five years, were set up to handle the development aid the Common Market countries promised their former colonies when they became associates of the Common Market. The first, with a capital of 581 million dollars (1958–63), was given away in direct development grants to former French, Belgian and Italian colonies in Africa. The orientation of this development fund was completely colonial, as the funds were distributed exclusively to the colonies and the new states on a prearranged basis.

The second development fund was established after all the African associates of the Common Market became independent by 1963. The Six re-negotiated the new agreement on a basis of equality with the eighteen African states and incorporated the results of these negotiations in the Yaounde Convention, placing the responsibility for submitting projects on the African states themselves and giving all members of the Community a say in their approval. The new development Fund began operations in June, 1964.

Under the new agreement, 680 million dollars of the development fund would be provided as outright grants; 50 million dollars for low-cost loans, and a further 70 million for normal-priced loans to be handled by the European Investment Bank. Provision was also made for various technical and scholarship programmes and the supply of European technical advisers, and assistance for manufacturing and productive industries.

It is significant to note that under the new fund 500 million dollars was allocated to general economic and social investment and technical assistance and the remaining 230 million dollars was earmarked for production aids and crop diversification.

Up to January, 1966, the new European Development Fund for the eighteen Associated African states was committed thus:

Rural modernisation	111	million dollars
Roads	31	,, ,,
Other infrastructure	21	,, ,,
Health	22	,, ,,
Education	14	,, ,,
Industrialisation	$1\frac{1}{2}$	,, ,,
Surveys	$6\frac{1}{2}$	,, ,,
Total:	207	million dollars

Because of her long association with most of these new states, France reaps more political benefits from this fund than, say, West Germany, which contributes the same 33 per cent of the Fund as France does. France picks up some 70 per cent of the development contracts while West Germany gets a mere 6 per cent. So far as the African countries are concerned, states like the Ivory Coast, Madagascar and Senegal, which have more sophisticated economies, benefit from the fund more than those with less developed economies.

Having discussed at some length the aid programmes of West Germany and the European Economic Community, we should now take a look at what is being done on the other side of the Atlantic by Canada, a relative newcomer into the field of economic and technical aid.

African confidence in the basic friendliness of Canada towards her aspirations was registered during the hectic days of the Congo–Kinshasa rebellion between 1960 and 1962. Canada supported the policies of the late Dag Hammarksjoeld and, later, U Thant, Secretaries-General of the United Nations, by supplying the bilingual telecommunications personnel for the whole United Nations Force in the Congo operations.

Another interesting Canadian intervention in the military field in Africa since the Congo crisis was the swift decision by the Canadian Government to step in after West Germany's rigid application of the Hallstein Doctrine in Tanzania led to the suspension or stoppage of several West German economic aid programmes in that country. Currently, Canada's military aid programmes are concentrated in *four* states:

(a) In Ghana, a military training mission of 30 officers has been maintained since 1961.

(b) Canada has offered Nigeria places for 22 officer cadets in the Canadian army and navy for further training.

(c) In addition to the Royal Canadian Air Force training of Tanzanian pilots, the Canadian Government has provided places for 12 officer cadets to take up army training in Canada.

   The construction of a military academy has also been planned by the Canadian military mission for Tanzania.

(d) Two officer cadets from Zambia were trained by the Canadian army.

Canada extends considerable aid to Africa through her programme, the Special Commonwealth African Assistance

Plan (SCAAP) for the building of secondary schools, trade training centres, forest inventory survey, natural gas feasibility study, aerial mapping and geophysics survey, and communications and technical services in Sierra Leone, Ghana, Nigeria, Kenya, Tanzania and the United Arab Republic.

Dr Hugh Moran, Director-General of the External Aid Office in Ottawa, summed up Canada's purpose in extending aid to the African countries in these words: "Our aim is to teach the teachers."

Dr Moran's office in Ottawa works on the sensible principle that Canada should emphasise those fields of aid in which she can offer special expertise: aerial mapping, fisheries development, mining surveys, hydro-electric power, statistical methods and scientific agriculture. The External Affairs Minister, Mr Martin, further explained Canada's purpose in extending aid to the new states. Canada's aid, he said, must never be used as a 'means of imposing our political views and attitudes on the developing countries—that would be self-defeating'. Mr Martin believes that the humanitarian motive must be foremost in the minds of Canadians, 'thus flagrant disparities in human wealth and welfare are no longer morally acceptable within a single community or the world community. So long as the world remains unequally divided into areas of affluence and indigence there cannot be expectation of true international peace and stability.'[4]

Canada's purposes in extending aid to the new states of Africa contrast vividly with those of the countries of the Sino-Soviet bloc as the utterances of the Communists clearly testify.

The former Soviet premier, Nikita Khruschev, in his address to the 22nd Party Congress of the Communist Party of the USSR, acclaimed his country's alliance with the young nation states of Asia, Africa and Latin America as the pillar of international politics for countries within the power orbit of the Sino-Soviet bloc. According to Mr Khruschev, foreign aid is to be one of the props of this alliance. To the Soviet bloc, however, the concept of foreign aid as a form of friendship carries a far broader meaning than as the West understands it. The Eastern bloc, which counts all types of aid, including cultural, as foreign economic aid, divides its programmes into four main sectors, namely:

1. Foreign trade as the 'foremost in economic collaboration' and a form of aid;
2. Credits and non-repayable aid;
3. Techno-scientific collaboration-building of plants and installations, research and planning, technical services and furnishing of specialists; and
4. Cultural collaboration and training aid.

Soviet bloc experts consider foreign trade the most important form of foreign aid because, as a concomitant of 'competition with capitalism' it sets the stage for the penetration of the developing nations' economies and the domination of their markets. Soviet loans are used in paying for equipment and materials purchased in the Soviet bloc. The Soviets consider such loans as a form of export subsidy. A Soviet article —the *Underdeveloped Countries in the Capitalistic Economy* states:

'Quite aside from their great importance, foreign loans and technical assistance actually serve only the ancillary function of raising the economy of the backward countries. The latter can be most effectively assisted through establishment of mutually profitable trade relations.'

The Soviet expert, A. Kodachenko, even more cogently expresses the position in these words:

'Foreign trade is one of the most important, and one of the most promising, forms of economic collaboration between under-developed countries of Asia, Africa and Latin America, and the USSR and other socialist states. The credits granted by the Soviet Union under the terms of its trade and aid agreements with the under-developed nations serve as a potent stimulus for Soviet exports to these states. Not only do these credits, as noted in the United Nations World Economy survey of 1958, create conditions favourable for continuous exchange of raw materials against manufactured goods supplied by countries operating under a centrally planned economy, but they may have an important effect on future exports to these under-developed nations.'[5]

Thus the Soviet Union's experts on foreign aid do not pretend to be doing any favours to the new states of Africa by extending foreign aid to them. All they want is to create favourable conditions for the export of their own manufactured goods. That this is a correct interpretation of Soviet foreign aid is supported by the words of no less an authority than Professor A. M. Smirnov. In his book, *USSR International Currency and Credit Relations* (1960, page 275), he states:

'To the USSR, granting of credits and other aid to the backward nations is not a charitable undertaking but assistance on a commercial basis.'

It is when Soviet propagandists twist this perfectly frank statement of their 'foreign aid' aims that some gullible Africans, including even some who pretend to be leaders, are taken in and, in turn, mislead their own nations.

What should be described as the Soviet Union's active participation in the field of foreign aid came only after Premier Khruschev signalled the green light at the Twentieth Party Congress in 1956:

'For the build-up of their independent national economy, as for the improvement of their people's standard of living, these under-developed nations may draw on the successes of the socialist world system, even though they are not members. Today they no longer need plead with their former oppressors for modern industrial equipment. Such equipment is available to them in the socialist countries, with no political or military strings attached.'[6]

Soviet propagandists dress up their foreign aid programmes politically as expressions of that peaceful economic competition which marks the current epoch of international relations.

Industrialisation is the magic word in the new states of Africa. Soviet propagandists know this too well and play upon the susceptibilities of the new nations. For this reason, Soviet foreign aid programmes stress projects such as giant industries which they hope will transform the economies of the backward nations overnight. Examples of such giant projects are the Aswan High Dam in Egypt and the Bhilai Steel Works in India. Soviet experts stress the point time and time again that their foreign aid programmes aim at bringing about speedy industrialisation and the construction of industrial works on the model of those in the older industrialised nations, and that their foreign aid programmes are given on a government-to-government basis so as to strengthen government influence in the new states as the lasting basis of true independence.

In the political sphere, Soviet experts hope that the establishment of large-scale industrial works will promote the emergence of a working class proletariat or a modern industrial labour force destined to lead the class struggle in these new countries and eventually replace the current leadership. A Soviet writer, Konrad Illgen, confirms this when he declares: 'An important aspect of industrialisation is the strengthening of the working class. The latter, led by its revolutionary party and imbued with a deep knowledge of the laws of social revolution, is particularly fit to accomplish the aims of the struggle for freedom and to safeguard the fruits of the democratic revolution.'[7]

Despite these prescriptions for large-scale industrialisation, Soviet experts have conceded defeat because of the peculiar and unfamiliar circumstances prevailing in most African countries. Professor I. I. Potekin admitted in his publication, *Africa 1956–61*, among other things, that 'for the smaller countries, recently become independent, this procedure [building of industrial plants] is practically impossible for the time being, in several cases not even desirable. Of 50 African territories only eight have a population of more than 10 million. It is self-evident that not all branches of industry can, or should, be developed in countries of limited population. Natural resources must also be considered.'

The Soviet prescription for the resolution of their dilemma is the establishment of an African Common Market.

Soviet bloc aid programmes include two types of loans: medium and long-term credits for specific projects and credits in a freely convertible currency. The Soviet bloc concentrates on the former type of loan, negotiated with recipient countries in Africa. Such agreements are usually called 'Agreements for Economic and Technical Collaboration'.

The interesting thing about these agreements is that the documents never contain firm, long-term price determinations. They are merely skeleton documents leaving the prices to be fixed 'on the basis of world market prices'. In every case, such agreements are later fleshed out with codicils, contracts and protocols, which at long last fix concrete prices. Officials in the developing countries complain that these subsequent price-fixing instruments are not only negotiated separately for each and every single project concerned, but additionally for every single aid category. For example, the price-fixing negotiations must cover the delivery of contracts, contracts for technical assistance, protocols for supplying specialists and for the training of local technicians.

A typical example of a Soviet agreement for Economic and Technical Collaboration is that with the Ghana Government. On August 4, 1960, the Soviet Union entered into a skeleton agreement with the Ghana Government. On December 23, 1960, a codicil was added, fixing the individual projects to be collaborated on by the Soviet and Ghanaian organisations, but no prices were fixed. The price-fixing was done consequently in each specific case in separate contracts on the basis of the following codicilliary stipulation:

'These contracts shall determine the volume, prices, delivery dates, and other conditions for the delivery of equipment and materials and for the services that are required by the terms of the Agreement here in question.'[8]

The catch in this type of communist agreement is that by the time the price-fixing exercise is concluded the final price to be paid by the recipient country is so inflated that the country becomes hopelessly entangled in debt. And yet another factor on which Soviet negotiators rely in making such agreements is the probability that the negotiators of the new states would not be sharp and alert enough to assess accurately the complicated clauses which they so cleverly insert into these instruments. The re-negotiation of several such agreements between the Soviet Union and the Ghana Government after the February 24, 1966 *coup d'état* vividly illustrates this point.

Between 1958 and 1964, the Soviet Union provided foreign aid funds totalling 1,642 million dollars to 14 countries in Africa. The projects covered by these loans range from the 350 million dollars granted to Egypt for the construction of the Aswan High Dam to the 12·2 million-dollar loan to Congo-Brazzaville for the construction of a drinking water supply system, a hydro-electric plant with a capacity of 1,500 to 2,000 kW, for geological prospecting, and the construction of a hotel in Brazzaville. Most of these loans carry an interest rate of 2·5 per cent.

Beside loans, the Soviet Union has distributed a number of 'free' gifts to the new states of Africa. In most cases, these 'gifts' are in effect barter agreements between the Soviet Union and the recipient country as the case of Burma illustrates. On January 17, 1957, the Soviet people presented to Burma a technological institute for 1,000 ordinary and 100 auditing students, a 200-bed hospital with polyclinic; a 180-seat theatre, a cultural-athletic centre with stadium and swimming pool; an industrial exhibition hall with a conference room for 1,000 people, and a hotel. The text of the agreement for this 'gift', we are informed, in *Friendly Aid and Mutually Profitable Collaboration* (Moscow, 1959, page 42) says that 'in return for the Soviet people's gift of friendship the Burmese Government has agreed to deliver to the USSR in the form of a present a corresponding amount of rice and goods of Burmese manufacture. These goods shall be delivered to the USSR within twenty years after completion of construction of the above facilities.'

The Soviet Union has distributed such free gifts to several countries in Africa. Of course, Heads of State are not forgotten in this operation. They receive Lenin Peace Prizes, airplanes, and libraries for their universities. All these gifts are, of course, without strings attached, except the natural one which any recipient of such largess feels—a soft attitude towards the donor.

By the end of 1965, China granted loans amounting to 842 million dollars to needy countries in Asia, Africa and Latin America. Of this amount, 627·5 million or 74·5 per cent were interest-free loans, 139·8 million or 16·6 per cent were donations and 74·7 million or 8·9 per cent carry 2·0–2·5 per cent interest. The Chinese policy of granting free loans or loans with very low interest rates is aimed at the Soviet Union as a weapon in the ideological warfare between the two Communist giants in their struggle to win the support of the new states of Asia, Africa and Latin America.

However, there is one interesting side of China's aid programmes to the new states which has a distinct advantage over Soviet aid. The Chinese, perhaps as a result of their own bitter experiences in concentrating on heavy industry, advised African states not to put all their aid funds into the establishment of large industrial enterprises.

The Chairman of the China Committee for the Development of International Trade, Non Han-tchen, said at the Algiers conference on February 23, 1965:

'One has to pay careful attention to the distribution of investments and their economic results. In principle it is preferable to make large investments in profitable than in non-profitable undertakings. . . . The economic results of the investments are inevitably lowered if the objective conditions are disregarded and the main emphasis is put on large-scale modern undertakings and the planning of self-contained complexes.'

Though Soviet propaganda continues to lambast Western economic aid as neo-colonialist, it encourages recipient countries to use them carefully under strictly planned economies. This is good advice which most of the developing countries must heed. Too often the ordinary people in the new states of Africa are deceived by the propaganda of their own leaders that development funds can be provided free or that they can secure loans from the Communist bloc 'without strings attached'. As illustrated by the examples of Soviet foreign aid agreements and other 'free gifts', the time has now come for the leaders of the new states to disabuse the minds of their nationals on this matter.

The success of every economic plan, as we have pointed out, depends on making the right choices at the critical moment. One dangerous lesson which the leaders of our new states have taught the ordinary citizens is that some things are free. The people have been taught in a number of countries that under African socialism or in the Welfare State the people must be provided free education, free medical and health services, free land and other free social services.

The time has surely come to explode this 'free' conception of social services, particularly as the concept applies to implementation of development programmes and disbursement of foreign loans. The ordinary citizens must be taught that nothing can be provided free for their enjoyment. The new leaders must be honest and realistic enough to explain to the illiterate sector of the population in every country that what they mean by 'free' education is actually subsidised education. This subsidy is provided by the richer members of the community who pay higher taxes, over and above what is regarded as equitable, so that the poorer citizens can enjoy the so-called free education, medical services and other free social services.

Also, the ordinary people must be educated to know that the so-called free social services are paid for out of the pockets of the richer members of the community who pay purchase tax on the luxury goods they buy, and that it is the taxes collected from this sector of the population that go to subsidise the free social services which all enjoy in the country. But above all, the ordinary people must be educated to realise that a time will come when they too, as their lot improves economically, must pay taxes to provide these 'free' social services for the rest of the community of which they also form a part.

'Free' social services are desirable in all African countries because the lot of the ordinary Africans must be improved so that they too can share in the fruits of independence. But the ordinary people must be prepared against the day when they too must pay part of the bill.

The second task facing African leaders is to explode the popular myth that there is something called foreign aid 'without strings attached'.

At best this popular myth is nothing but a hollow political slogan that fools nobody. Foreign donors are not in the business for pleasure, as the Russian Professor Smirnov, frankly stated. Foreign donors extend aid to the new states not only to get a rich return on their investment, particularly in the private sector, but also to help the developing nations to raise their own standards of living, thus creating new demands for their manufactured commodities.

The leaders of the new states must, therefore, educate their compatriots to realise that so far as bilateral loans are concerned, there are *always* strings attached. Even in case of multilateral economic aid projects, the international agencies involved do not just pour money down waste-pipes. They undertake feasibility studies to satisfy themselves that any capital advanced for the implementation of such projects would not be wasted. These feasibility studies are the strings attached to the aid sought.

It is good sense that all aid with political strings attached should be rejected. At the same time, the ordinary people must be told the truth about foreign aid, namely that all such aid has strings attached, in one form or the other, notwithstanding the assertions of Communist propagandists and their African stooges to the contrary.

6
The Search for African Unity

As WE HAVE seen in the previous chapter, aid from the industrialised nations to the developing countries of Africa is a symbol of their realisation that we all belong to a world community and that to ensure peace and stability in this one world the developing nations must not be permitted to remain forever perpetually poor and miserable. Some of the leaders of the new states keenly appreciate their membership of this world community and for this reason took steps immediately after attaining independence to forge links with their neighbours. They also became members of the United Nations.

Several attempts were made by African leaders in the late 1950s and early 1960s to form regional groupings as the nucleus of a larger union of African independent states. The earliest was the Ghana-Guinea Union of November 23, 1958. The two leaders, former President Kwame Nkrumah of Ghana and President Sekou Touré of Guinea, signed a document setting out the basic principles of the Union of Independent African States envisaging union citizenship, an Economic Council and a Union Bank. This Ghana-Guinea Union was followed by several others such as the Mali Federation of Senegal and Soudan which broke up in August, 1960, the Ghana-Guinea-Mali Union of December 24, 1960, the Brazzaville group, the *Conseil de l'Entente* of Ivory Coast, Upper Volta, Niger and Dahomey and later, the Monrovia group of states. All these regional groups were the forerunners of the larger organisation, the Organisation for African Unity, which was born on May 25, 1963, in Addis Ababa, the Ethiopian capital.

The OAU was established to promote, among other things, the unity and solidarity of the African and Malagasy states

and to co-ordinate and intensify their co-operation and efforts
to achieve a better life for the peoples of the continent. Its
aims and purposes are similar to those of the United Nations,
a world organisation to which all members of the OAU
belong. The question has, therefore, been asked why the
African states duplicated the United Nations by the founding
of the OAU. The answer to this question explains the reasons
for the formation of the OAU, its development so far and
the dilemmas and problems it has had to face since its
birth.

The OAU is a child of strife, born out of the ideological
clash between the Casablanca group of states—Ghana,
Guinea, Mali, the United Arab Republic, Morocco and the
Algerian Provisional Government in Exile—and the Monrovia group of states—most of the Francophone states and
the Anglophone states of Liberia, Nigeria, Sierra Leone,
Ethiopia, Somalia and Tanganyika (Tanzania).

During the latter part of 1960, the Casablanca group of
states propagated the idea of an immediate formation of an
African Continental Government, and an African High Command. The Continental Government envisaged was to be a
political union of African states with an Executive Cabinet,
a continental Parliament of a Lower House and a Senate
and a military force under an African High Command. The
Casablanca group of states became known as the radical
states because of their loud claim that they were the 'true re-
volutionaries'.

As a foil to the claims of this radical group, the moderate
states met in Monrovia in 1961 to propagate the idea of
African union through step-by-step economic collaboration.

One main difference between the Monrovia and the Casa-
blanca groups of states was expressed by former President
Nnamdi Azikiwe of the Nigerian Federation at their second
Lagos conference in January, 1962, in these words:

> 'One basic difference was the conspicuous absence of a
> specific declaration on the part of the Casablanca states of
> their inflexible belief in the fundamental principles enunciated

at Monrovia regarding the inalienable right of African states as at present constituted to legal equality, irrespective of their area and population.

'Other principles ignored by the Casablanca powers are the right to self-determination, safety from interference in their internal affairs, and safety from external aggression.'[1]

Dr Azikiwe said that although these principles were embodied in the United Nations Charter it was important for African unity that the African states should declare publicly and recapitulate their faith and firm belief in the principles laid down at Monrovia. The unity the Lagos conference sought, he said, was one based *NOT* on regimental uniformity. Total unity was impossible in Africa as in any other continent, but Africa could develop unity in diversity and channel diversity in unity.

(Subsequent events proved that Dr Azikiwe was a better prophet than perhaps he himself realised in 1962. He pinpointed the philosophical differences between the radical and moderate states—differences which were to plague the political policies of the OAU in subsequent years, particularly in the resolution of the Congo crises between 1964 and 1965.)

It was obvious by the beginning of 1963 that there were too many political and economic groupings of African states, all trying to achieve the same goal, African Unity. In the meantime, some of the states mounted a vicious campaign of vilification against each other through their mass media of communication, and some promoted subversive activities against what they described as 'neo-colonialist' states. By March, 1963, it became clear, even to the politically blind, that the enmity between the several states was threatening to blow up the continent in a senseless fratricidal war.

It was at this juncture that Emperor Haile Selassie of Ethiopia proposed a conference of the Heads of State and Governments in his capital, Addis Ababa, to resolve the differences between the various warring factions. The Organisation of African Unity was born at this conference.

The Founding Fathers of the OAU took great care in spelling out the purposes and aims of the organisation in clear and unmistakable language. They also established the institutions that would promote the purposes and implement the aims of the organisation. These were all inscribed in the Charter which all Heads of State signed. It was hoped that with the new organisation African unity could be forged within the lifetime of most of the signatories, thus bringing an end to the inter-state rivalries, abuses and subversion against each member state. These hopes were to be bitterly shattered.

Perhaps what the Founding Fathers forgot to consider seriously during the negotiations were the political hostilities and suspicions between the radical and moderate states, the economic disparities between the states and the inordinate ambitions of certain Heads of State and their dictatorial and contemptuous attitudes towards other Heads of State. It was the lackadaisical manner in which these differences were glossed over during the founding of the organisation that later contributed to the problems of the OAU and the split in the organisation into two hostile camps on the eve of the Heads of State conference in Accra in 1965.

These major differences can be categorised thus:

1. lack of consensus among the states about the definition of the concept of 'non-alignment';
2. the handling of the Congo and Rhodesian crises;
3. reaction of member states towards the spate of military *coups d'état* in various African states;
4. organised subversion against fellow member states by some Heads of State; and
5. methods of achieving continental unity, especially due to the emergence of one-party states in numerous African countries.

The failure of the Heads of State and the Council of Ministers, who incidentally passed the buck to the Heads of State, to define what exactly is meant by non-alignment is the result of the old rivalry between the radical Casablanca and the moderate Monrovia groups of state. The radicals believe in and preach what they call scientific socialism. In their anxiety to cut their links with the former metropolitan powers, they tend to lean towards the Eastern Sino-Soviet power bloc, no doubt believing that imported ideologies and slogans will solve all their socio-economic problems. The moderates, especially the more conservative ones, believe in maintaining the *status quo*, not because they abhor change *per se*, but they also believe, no doubt genuinely, that they can solve their socio-economic problems in a more orderly and systematic fashion by maintaining their old links with the former colonial masters. This is particularly true of the Francophone states whose economies, as we have seen in the previous chapter, largely depend on massive subventions and economic aid from France particularly and the Six of the European Economic Community.

The inability to establish a consensus over non-alignment is not merely a matter of semantics. It goes deeper than that. During 1965, for instance, it helped to intensify the divisive forces between the states, particularly in their reaction towards such vexed questions as relations with Communist China, the breaking of diplomatic relations with Britain over the Rhodesian unilateral declaration of independence, and the subversive activities mounted against some Francophone states by ex-President Nkrumah of Ghana.

The manner in which the OAU as a body handled the Congo crisis of July, 1964, up to the dethronement of former Congolese Prime Minister Moise Tshombe in November, 1965, by President Joseph Mobutu demonstrated, as nothing else had, the deep divisions among the several states and the confusion prevailing over the interpretation of Article III of the Charter of the Organisation laying down the principle of sovereign equality of all member states and non-interference in the internal affairs of these states.

After the United Nations withdrew from the Congo-Kinshasa on June 30, 1964, the long-expected civil strife broke. Rebel bands under communist-trained Congolese such as Gaston Soumialot, Christophe Gbenye and Pierre Mulele, staged an armed rebellion against the Central Government of ex-President Joseph Kasavubu and Prime Minister Cyrille Adoula. The Central Government was clearly unable to stem the tide of this civil strife. To the consternation of all outsiders, President Kasavubu invited Moise Tshombe who had master-minded the Katanga secessionist movement in 1960, the 'political leper' of the OAU, to head a Provisional Government of National Pacification in Kinshasa (Leopoldville). The recall of Mr Tshombe provoked Gaston Soumialot to announce the formation of a Provisional Government of the National Committee of Liberation on July 23, 1964. His rebel bands captured Kinsangani (Stanleyville) on August 5, 1964, and the rebellion became a full-scale guerrilla war.

In the midst of this new crisis, Moise Tshombe took complete control of the Central Government in Kinshasa. He recruited European mercenaries, most of them his old Katanga veterans, to lead the Congolese National Army under General Joseph Mobutu to war against the rebel forces of Soumialot, Gbenye and Mulele.

Under the Charter of the OAU and that of the United Nations, to which all member states subscribed, the OAU states had no choice but to support the Central Government of the Congo, no matter who headed it. To admit this principle was too much for some of the radical states because of their abhorence of Mr Tshombe, who, they believed, was responsible for the murder of Patrice Lumumba, the Congo's first Prime Minister. This rejection of Tshombe as Prime Minister of the Congo split the OAU wide open when it was summoned to debate the Congo crisis.

The Stanleyville operation, mounted by the American, British and Belgian governments on November 22–24 for the rescue of hostages, hardened the attitude of the OAU states, particularly the radical ones, towards Mr Tshombe. The Americans were condemned for providing the planes; the Belgians, the commandos; the British for providing a staging point on Ascension Island. The radical states, notably the United Arab Republic and Algeria, provided direct military aid for the Congolese rebels; the Sudan, Uganda and Congo-Brazzaville provided sanctuary and staging points in their territories for the rebel troops so as to facilitate infiltration into the Congo; and Ghana, Guinea, Mali, Tunisia and Morocco declared themselves against Mr Tshombe's premiership. Most of the Francophone states at first kept mute but later openly supported the premiership of Mr Tshombe.

The Congo crisis which the OAU *Ad Hoc* Committee under President Kenyatta of Kenya failed to resolve, the stern denunciation of the Stanleyville rescue operation by the African states at home and at the United Nations, and the abandonment of the principle of equal sovereignty of member states split the OAU down the middle. The organisation is still suffering from the results of this split.

The unilateral declaration of independence by the Prime Minister of Rhodesia on November 11, 1965, three weeks after the OAU summit conference in Accra, contributed towards the ideological split in the OAU. Although the OAU states were unanimous in their condemnation of Mr Smith's rebellion, there was no unanimity as to how to deal with this affront to African dignity, and the defiance of Great Britain committed by the Smith regime. While some states talked of military intervention, others argued that Britain should be given a chance to settle the crisis.

At an extraordinary meeting of Council of Ministers held at Addis Ababa on December 3, 1965, the radicals won the day and a resolution was adopted asking that if Mr Smith did not purge himself of his treason by abandoning his unilateral declaration of independence the OAU states would mount a military action against Rhodesia, cut all economic and communications links with the colony and break off diplomatic relations with Britain. Though the resolution to break off diplomatic relations with Britain was unanimously adopted only a few of the states kept their word when the time-limit expired. The nine states that actually broke their diplomatic links with Britain were Ghana, Guinea, Tanzania, the United Arab Republic, the Sudan, Mali, Mauritania, Congo-Brazzaville and Algeria.

The various military coups of late 1965 and early 1966 further helped to strain the relations between the radicals and moderates in OAU.

It all began when General Joseph Mobutu deposed 'King' Kasavubu on November 25, 1965, to thwart a much-publicised *détente* with Congo-Brazzaville across the River.

On December 22, General Christophe Soglo of Dahomey, for the second time in three years, ousted the wrangling politicians and took over to prevent his small, poverty-stricken country from total economic collapse.

The epidemic of military takeovers reached the Central African Republic on December 31–January 1, when Colonel Jean Bokasa deposed his cousin, President David Dacko, ostensibly to thwart a Chinese-Communist managed subversive plot against the Dacko regime.

On January 4, 1966, the military deposed President Maurice Yameogo of the Upper Volta.

The Nigerian military staged a confused *coup d'état* on January 15, the very day a Commonwealth Prime Ministers' conference on the Rhodesian crisis had ended in Lagos. Eventually Major-General John Ironsi emerged as the victor.

The Nigerian coup shook the very foundations of African unity principally because of the murder of Sir Abubakar Tafawa Balewa, the Federal Prime Minister, who was considered as a leader of the moderate group of states at the level of the OAU.

On February 24, 1966, the unbelievable happened. The noisy, demanding, power-drunk, corrupt and seemingly impregnable Kwame Nkrumah of Ghana was deposed in a classic army-cum-police operation. The Redeemer himself was out of the country on a self-appointed peace mission to Hanoi.

Each of these coups was caused by the political and the socio-economic conditions peculiar to each country. However, the military leaders, particularly those of Ghana and the Central African Republic, were also apprehensive of the pro-Chinese communist tendencies in their countries. These coup leaders were anxious to have more co-operation with the former metropolitan powers so as to stem the tide of poverty in each country.

One interesting result of the series of military coups was the strengthening of the position of the moderates in the councils of the OAU. This was clearly demonstrated when there was confusion and long argument over the sitting of the Ghana delegation at the Ministerial Council conference at Addis Ababa on February 28, 1966. Ten radical states walked out of the conference because they considered the new military regime in Accra unconstitutional. This show of temper on the part of the radical states was a mere repetition of the same confusion which prevailed in Cairo in 1964 when Mr Tshombe appeared as the Prime Minister of the Congo-Leopoldville.

The signatories of the OAU Charter pledged themselves unreservedly to 'condemn, in all its forms, political assassinations, as well as subversive activities on the part of neighbouring states or any other states'. This pledge is one of the cardinal principles governing the relationships between member states of the organisation. It was expected, therefore, that whatever the disagreements between the various states, their leaders would eschew subversion as a means of settling their differences. It is a matter of record that this wise principle was violated with impunity by a number of Governments who believed that continental unity could be achieved overnight and on their terms only.

In a speech delivered by President Hamani Diori of Niger in January, 1965, to a meeting of the *Conseil de l'Entente*, he said that their regional organisation was being rejuvenated to combat 'the siege of Africa by Chinese communism'. The siege of Africa by Chinese communism to which President

Diori referred was not new. It was part and parcel of the original suspicion between the radical and moderate states and their quarrel over the importation of foreign ideologies into Africa.

Member states of the *Conseil de l'Entente* accused the Government of former President Nkrumah of training subversive elements in military camps in Ghana to overthrow their regimes, mainly because of ideological differences. After the February 24, 1966, *coup d'état* in Ghana these allegations against the Nkrumah regime were confirmed in every particular when the new regime closed the military training camps and sent home the Chinese communist instructors brought in by Nkrumah to train African saboteurs.

During the last two years of his regime, 1964–65, Nkrumah did his best to impose his visionary ideas of continental union on the rest of the leaders of Africa. He believed firmly that it was only through the establishment of a Continental Union Government that all the economic, social and political problems of the continent could be solved. Nkrumah's propagandists sold the idea energetically throughout Africa, Europe and the Americas. The enslaved Ghana press and radio trumpeted the idea day and night and his 'gaping sycophants', the Ministers of State, took good care that they did not deliver a single speech without stating the fact that Continental Union Government must be achieved soon.

It was Nkrumah's belief that the only effective way to defeat 'neo-colonialism' was to form an African continental government. He says in his last book, *Neo-Colonialism the Last Stage of Imperialism*, page 259:

'African unity is something which is within the grasp of the African people. The foreign firms who exploited our resources long ago saw the strength to be gained from acting on a Pan-African scale. By means of interlocking directorships, cross-shareholdings and other devices, groups of apparently different companies have formed, in fact, one enormous capitalist monopoly. The only effective way to challenge this economic empire and to recover possession of our heritage is for us also to act on a Pan-African basis, through a Union Government.'

The hypocrisy of the Nkrumah regime, his subversive activities against his neighbours in West Africa, and the propagandistic activities of his numerous paid stooges in other African countries caused his desperate call for the formation of a Union Continental Government to fall on deaf ears.

The moderate states, for these and other good reasons, advocated economic, cultural and social collaboration as prerequisites of the formation of political union step by step. For political and economic reasons some of the moderate states were and are still suspicious of the raucous call of the radical states for the formation of an immediate continental government. Some Heads of State are apprehensive that if they were to deliver their nationals to the tender mercies of a supra-national Government they themselves would be swept away quickly and their fellow country men and women would be enslaved by the vociferous radicals.

Former President Azikiwe of Nigeria gave voice to these fears in an article in the first issue of the US magazine, *African Forum*:

> 'If the citizen of an African state can be assured that his worth as an individual is respected by the state; that he can enjoy his constitutional rights and fulfil his civic obligations as a citizen under the rule of law; that he will be ruled by a Government chosen by a majority in a society of which he is a member; where he will be free to express his opinions without fear or favour, subject to the due process of law; that such a Government will be a true reflection of the collective will of his community, to serve for a stated tenure and to wield power in trust for the community until an election that will be free and fair determine his future rulers then such a citizen should willingly support the surrender of the sovereignty of his state to that of a United States of Africa.'

With the numerous one-party states, draconian Preventive Detention Acts on the statute books of several of them, and the mock trials that go for justice in several countries, not only the Heads of State but ordinary African citizens do not feel happy about the prospects of a Continental Union Government under which there would be no place to hide.

The inability of the OAU to solve some of its political problems is due not to any fundamental defects in the Charter or even the institutions established under the Charter but to the conflicting ideologies and the clash of personalities who have sought to dominate the organisation. The impotence of the organisation is also partly due to the inability of the Heads of State and Council of Ministers to differentiate between fact and fiction, principle and expediency, emotionalism and reality, slogans and sobriety. In the Congo crisis mentioned above, principle demanded that the OAU support the then legal Government of the Congo, no matter who headed it. This principle was abandoned because of emotional attachment to the departed Patrice Lumumba and the belief in the fiction that the rebels of Soumialot and Gbenye still controlled the Congo in face of the Stanleyville operation.

In the Rhodesian crisis, African leaders felt frustrated because of their military impotence. Most of them knew too well that they could not mount a successful military operation against the rebellious regime of Mr Smith since they could not support an invading army with their lines of communication and paucity of military hardware. In face of these facts some leaders propagated the fiction that the 'socialist states'—meaning Communist China and the Soviet Union— would come to their aid once hostilities against Rhodesia were launched. Thus by abandoning principle, resorting to emotionalism, adhering to fictitious and unrealistic positions on some matters and by preaching empty slogans as the panacea for all the ills and woes of Africa, the organisation continues to display childishness in major crisis and fails to live up to the great expectations that swept the continent at its birth.

And yet the OAU has scored some triumphs since its inception. These include the settling of the border claims between Algeria and Morocco in 1963, the police action in the

Congo under the aegis of the United Nations between 1960–64, and recent *rapprochment* between Kenya and Somalia over the disputed Northern Frontier District of Kenya. In the technical fields, it has sponsored several studies in communications and transport which are expected to yield fruits in the years to come. The OAU has collaborated with the United Nations Economic Commission for Africa in many technical and economic matters for the betterment of the peoples of Africa, particularly in the establishment of the African Development Bank, with headquarters in Ivory Coast, a bank which is expected to provide much-needed funds for carrying out regional development projects for which money could not be raised through other international agencies.

All African leaders and peoples share the vision of a united Africa some day. But most believe that this unity cannot be achieved through deceit of member states or the citizens of the various countries. African unity will come one day, but it cannot come through the shouting of slogans. To achieve it, the citizens and leaders of the member states must learn to build bridges of understanding, tolerance and trust between each other.

Above all, Africa must produce men who have faith in Africa, men who will not import foreign ideologies into African relations so as to enslave the people. These are the men and women who can unite the Africa of tomorrow.

7
Foreign Policies of African States

THE APPEARANCE at the United Nations General Assembly in 1960 of a large number of newly independent states from Black Africa introduced a new type of diplomacy into the conduct of international affairs. The new states sounded a note of radicalism and directness which completely shocked the older nations. The urgency of the needs of these new states compels their representatives to adopt strident postures which contrast rudely with the slower, more subtle and formal diplomacy of the past. Sir Alec Douglas-Home, when British Foreign Secretary, had occasion in early 1962 to comment on this new development at the United Nations. He warned that the 'double standards' which the African representatives introduced into the UN would lead to its early disintegration if the practice persisted.

We noted in the last chapter that African states adopted this double standard in resolving some aspects of the Congo crisis in 1964 and did the same with the recognition of the Ghana delegation at the Ministerial Council meeting in Addis Ababa in February, 1966. There must then be some reason for this posture of African states in the conduct of their international relations.

Africa entered the councils of the world at a critical period in the life of the United Nations itself. When the United Nations was founded in 1945 it was mainly a club for European and Latin American nations, with a handful of independent Asian and African countries. Its deliberations concerned mainly the resolution of Cold War problems, the Middle East, and the general interplay of power politics.

Colonial and Trusteeship questions took second place in the world forum.

By 1960, the situation had changed dramatically when almost all the African Francophone states became independent and joined the United Nations. This event gave the 46-member Afro-Asian bloc a near-majority. Although by no means a solid front, these countries presented a common viewpoint on such subjects as condemnation of colonialism and racialism. Just as these new African states moved into the mainstream of world affairs, the Congo crisis plunged the United Nations into the heart of Africa, involving it more deeply than any event since the Korean war.

The Belgians did not leave the Congo too soon. They left it too suddenly. The Congo at Independence on June 30, 1960, was ill-prepared for the great adventure of self-government. There were only a handful of African administrators and not a single officer in the Congolese *Force Publique*. And yet nationalist propaganda had prepared the Congolese for stepping into the jobs of all Belgians. When independence came, the ill-disciplined Congolese troops refused to take orders from their Belgian officers and mutinied. A long nightmare of rioting and pillaging followed. In the chaotic events following the mutiny, Moise Tshombe, President of the Katanga Regional Assembly, steered by Belgian agents of the giant Union Minière du Haut Katanga announced the Province's secession from the new Republic of the Congo.

Unable to cope with these disastrous events, and unwilling to sacrifice his country's independence by calling back the Belgians who had already compromised their neutrality in the Katanga affair, the erratic but popular Premier, Patrice Lumumba, appealed to the United Nations Secretary-General, Dag Hammarksjoeld, for assistance. The United Nations complied by sending in troops from neutral Afro-Asian countries to police the Congo. At the same time the United Nations sent in a large team of administrators, physicians and technicians in all fields—telecommunications personnel, mostly Canadians and Ghanaians, teachers, policemen—all under the supervision of a fifteen-member advisory committee.

The United Nations also appointed a United Nations Commissioner, who was the Secretary-General's personal representative to the Congo, to keep essential welfare and government services going. The United Nations presence was maintained in the Congo for four chaotic, trying and desperate years.

It was this Congo experience which convinced the new states of Africa that their membership of the United Nations could be used as a lever to redress almost all the wrongs which the former colonial masters had inflicted on subject races in Africa and elsewhere. During the past seven years the African states have played their part in the liquidation of colonialism.

African leaders, both as representatives and nationalists, have sought at the United Nations to focus world attention on the struggles for justice and freedom, particularly in the remaining colonies, Mozambique, Angola, Portuguese Guinea, South West Africa and Somalia (French). It is in this campaign against colonialism and racialism that African states have clashed with the old nations in their formal, slower methods of diplomacy. The African representatives have no stomach for subtlety, fine words or patience when discussing colonial questions. They are convinced that where colonies remain the struggle for their liberation must be waged without compromise, no matter who gets hurt in the process.

Often the African leaders' expectations of United Nations action have been excessive. In the application of sanctions against South Africa and the rebellious regime of Ian Smith in Rhodesia, for example, most Africans expected the United Nations to employ military force. This expectation was due mainly to false interpretation of the Charter. But whether this false interpretation is deliberate or just a propaganda stance to impress the largely illiterate population in Africa is still difficult to unscramble.

The tactics of African leaders in the United Nations have

often been questionable. The most appalling manifestation of such questionable tactics was the African reaction to the rescue operation of November, 1964. Just before Stanleyville radio went off the air on November 24, it announced: 'Brethren, since Jomo Kenyatta has not come, sharpen your knives and your matchetes tomorrow to behead all the whites.' The orders were given in *Linguala*.

These orders were given by the leaders of the *Conseil National de Libération* (CNL) of Christophe Gbenye.

It was this threat to behead all the white hostages that forced the Belgians, Americans and the British to collaborate in mounting the rescue operation. Although this was a humanitarian undertaking, much irrational African talk in New York and in Africa did a great deal of harm to relations between Africa and Europe. The Stanleyville affair led to a complete breakdown of communication between Africans and non-Africans at the end of 1964.

Kenya's President Kenyatta, that level-headed statesman, told a sad story about the Stanleyville operation that blamed the United States for using force in the rescue operation. In an address to the OAU *Ad Hoc* Commission on the Congo just after the rescue operation, President Kenyatta said:

> 'I stood for the peaceful negotiations. I said on behalf of the OAU *Ad Hoc* Commission that I could promise to carry on the peaceful discussions and to effect sending a peaceful delegation from OAU countries. Mr Atwood [US Ambassador in Nairobi], on the other hand, stood for force. He told me that his idea was the quickest and that the most humanitarian way was to use force'.[1]

After the fall of Stanleyville, Algeria's Ben Bella said the Belgian humanitarian hostage lift was 'aggression' against the Congo. He warned that even though 'Stanleyville has fallen, Africa remains—the same Africa which groups the Congo, Algeria, Conakry and Cairo'. The Algerian Ambassador to Peking said: 'Although the city of Stanleyville has fallen, the patriots still exist. If necessary, they will utilise the latest experience to correct and improve the form of their struggle; they may carry on the struggle as we did in Algeria in the past.'

Three years after the Stanleyville affair it is still difficult to look at the matter objectively either through African or non-African eyes because of the great human tragedy it symbolised and the tragic picture it presents of African diplomacy, even where the interests of African lives are concerned. Thousands of African lives were saved by the hostage lift in Stanleyville but this humanitarian operation angered all African states more than any other single 'imperialist' action during the whole of 1964.

Often, the independent states of Africa pursue questionable policies which in the long run work against their own interests. One such policy is the expulsion of South Africa and Portugal from the technical commissions and Specialised Agencies of the United Nations operating in Africa.

In July, 1964, U Thant in a Geneva address to the meeting of the Economic and Social Council of the United Nations said the emergence of the less developed countries as a group of Seventy-five may well signal a turn in the history of international relations. The contribution to be expected from this group of Seventy-five, he said, would depend to a great extent on the validity of the United Nations as an instrument for reconciling differences of opinion and not only as a framework in which they could manifest themselves.

Developments at various international conferences since then have proved that most members of the group of Seventy-five do not consider the United Nations as an 'instrument for reconciling differences of opinion' but rather as a divisive, destructive instrument. A few weeks after U Thant made his Geneva speech a world conference on education was convened by UNESCO in Geneva. During the eight days of the conference not a single word was spoken on education. Instead, African, Asian and Eastern European communist politicians, most of them professional conference attenders, argued, shouted and tabled resolutions demanding the expulsion of Portugal from the conference. Their reason was that Portugal, a colonial power, had no right to attend such conferences until and unless she granted independence to her colonies, Mozambique, Angola and Guinea. When finally the issue of Portugal's expulsion was put to the vote, forty countries, mostly Western and Latin American, walked out of the conference and it collapsed.

The irony of the whole futile argument over Portugal's presence is that in all these African countries education has barely touched the fringes of the population. A UNESCO survey had it that there were about 750 million adult illiterates in the world. Africa's share of that total was between 94 and 104 million adult illiterates in 1964. The Geneva conference was specifically convened to consider the problem of illiteracy on a global basis and to make plans to tackle it in the 1970s. The Eastern European states which helped the Afro-Asian nations in voting for the ouster of Portugal have well-educated populations. And yet Afro-Asian politicians destroyed a grand opportunity to discuss education, a factor which plays a vital part in their efforts to abolish poverty and disease and helps in raising the standards of living of their hungry millions. If Portugal had been allowed to participate in the conference, she might have been forced to spend a little more money on the education of her African population and consequently speed up the process of her own liquidation as a colonial power in Africa, the very goal the Afro-Asians desire so fervently.

The same tactics have been applied to South Africa at various international gatherings. The latest was the walk-out staged in New Delhi at the February, 1968, conference of UNCTAD. There is no doubt that South Africa is the most advanced nation in Africa. She has the technical know-how and the human and financial resources to help some of the African states to improve their economies and solve some of their social problems. Her presence at international gatherings is not wanted because of her hated policy of *apartheid*.

Certain African leaders, notably Malawi's Dr Hastings Banda, have seen the absurdity of this anti-South African stance and have moved to open a dialogue with the racist regime. Dr Banda has been denounced by the more vociferous African nationalist leaders as a 'traitor to Africa' for establishing diplomatic relations with the South African regime. Such reckless denunciations do not help anybody, particularly the black Africans living in the *apartheid* Republic. Many sober-minded African leaders are beginning to see that they cannot forever continue to live in a dreamland. Some are beginning to grapple with realities. They are having second thoughts on their anti-South African attitude. These leaders are no less vehement than their peers in condemning the policy of *apartheid*, but they believe that the more their antagonism the more severe the restrictions she would impose on the black Africans in the Republic. The African realists would like to open a dialogue with her to see what could be done to persuade her to modify her policies.

Despite such occasional displays of strident postures at the United Nations, African representatives have succeeded through diplomacy in bringing about improvements in the living standards of their nationals through the activities of United Nations Specialised Agencies and the Economic Commission for Africa. The success of the ECA is a welcome departure from the sterile debates in older organs such as the Trusteeship Council and its Committee on Information on Non-Self-Governing Territories.

The ECA was created in 1958, the last of such regional economic councils, as a result of the demands of the new states of Africa, to make surveys and studies in co-operation with African states and to recommend joint utilisation of resources and techniques of economic development. Since its creation the ECA has been the central planning agency for the United Nations Technical Assistance Programme in Africa. It has spearheaded the establishment of regional economic communities, such as the East African Common

Market of Kenya, Uganda and Tanzania, the African Development Bank, the Administrative Training Institute in Dakar, and the East-Central African Economic Community. It has inspired the debates on the formation of the West African Economic Community, the Maghreb Economic Community and several technical organisations in the communications, transport and agricultural fields throughout Africa.

The activities of other Specialised Agencies of the United Nations such as the World Health Organisation, the Food and Agricultural Organisation, United Nations Educational, Scientific and Cultural Organisation (UNESCO) and the World Bank for Reconstruction and Development, have all contributed towards a better life in the new states. It was also the pressure of the Afro-Asian bloc that led to the creation of the International Development Agency, the UN Special Fund, the UN Capital Development Fund and the United Nations Conference on Trade and Development (UNCTAD).

Thus Africa, at her coming of age, is effectively using the United Nations as the primary arena in which the new relationships between the Western and Eastern powers and independent Africa will be evolved.

The dilemma which plagued the conduct of the foreign relations of these independent new states between the years 1960 and 1966 can be likened in parody, to Hamlet's soliloquy:

> *To lean or not to lean*
> *To the East or to the West?*
> *What a mess!*

The present rulers of the new states stepped into the shoes of the colonial powers through the administrative, legal and educational system and other trappings of sovereignty which they inherited from their former masters. The natural tendency was for them to practise what they had also learnt from their former mentors. Thus the Francophone states based their new administrations on the French colonial pattern as did the Anglophone ones on the British pattern. Alongside these colonial patterns and ideas, the new leaders developed their own concepts such as African socialism, Pan-Africanism, neutralism and non-alignment; nursed certain myths and beliefs, all of which determine their conduct of foreign relations.

So the radical states propagate the idea of continental political union as soon as possible while the moderate states prefer step-by-step collaboration in the economic and cultural fields as the basis for eventual continental political union.

These radical states differ from the moderate states also in the conduct of their foreign and inter-African relations. It is generally true to say that while the radical states are more intolerant of the views of others, the moderate states prefer to discuss all views before drawing their own conclusions.

African nationalism developed in two main directions after independence: micro-nationalism and macro-nationalism. According to this classification, first used by Senegal's ex-Foreign Minister, Dr Duoduo Thiam, the revolutionary or radical states usually tend to be macro-nationalists and the moderate or humanist states tend to be micro-nationalists.

The macro-nationalist leaders look at the continent as one political entity that must move in one direction, preferably under their guidance and dictation. For this reason they have been foremost in propagating the idea of immediate continental political union and have in some cases made territorial claims against their neighbours as in the cases of Algeria against Morocco, Ghana against Togo and the Ivory Coast and Somalia against Kenya and Ethiopia.

The macro-nationalist leaders have also used the concept of Pan-Africanism to fight communism in their own states, as a weapon in the fight against colonialism and the consolidation of independence and achieving African unity. Above all, the macro-nationalist leaders have tended to be intransigent, intolerant of moderation and have conducted their inter-African and foreign relations in the communist style.

The micro-nationalist leaders are sometimes referred to as the humanist socialist leaders who want to change African society, raise the standards of living of their nationals and promote African unity gradually. These states are moderate in their dealings with each other and foreign countries. They lean more to the Western power bloc in their international relations.

Despite the existence of the Organisation for African Unity and in spite of the fact that there are no major ideological disagreements between the Black African States, the differences of approach in practical conduct of foreign policy between the macro- and micro-nationalist states constitute a grave danger to Africa. That danger is the infiltration of Communism from Red China and Russia and other Eastern power bloc states, neo-colonialism from the West and the creation of black imperialism and repressive one-party states within Africa by Africans themselves.

These differences between the various African states have been manifested in their dealings with one another. They have been demonstrated in the African propensity for playing the diplomatic game according to their own rules, not only at the United Nations but also at the OAU, and between individual African states. The military coups of late 1965 and early 1966 have deposed some of the macro- and micro-nationalist leaders. The dismissal of some of these leaders has brought a new lease of life into inter-African relations and the strains and stresses that characterised inter-African and foreign diplomacy during the early days of independence have now been modified.

But the main problem remains: can African states remain really and factually non-aligned in their relations with foreign countries? Dr Thiam poses the question in these words:

> ' The non-alignment which everyone in Africa claims the right to exercise does not prevent and has not yet prevented

sympathies from going to one or the other of the blocs. Here we see the full extent of tne problem of Africa's future. Faced by the existing blocs, will Black Africa be able to work out a policy of its own, genuinely reflecting its personality and its soul?

'Pan-Africanism, African cultural consciousness, the African road to socialism, neutralism—will these provide an adequate protection against the millstones of alien ideologies between which Africa is gradually being caught? Or will the continent be divided, like Asia, between the various currents and trends, falling finally into the ideological and political grip of the giants of this world?'[2]

8

The Role of the Press in Africa

ALL THE LEADERS of the new nations of Africa are fighting the Four Horsemen of the United Nations: poverty, disease, ignorance and apathy. When these Four Horsemen are defeated the leaders will be in a position to raise the living standards of their countrymen and provide for them the 'more abundant life'. In this endeavour to improve living conditions in all African states, the Press—and indeed all media of mass communication—has a vital role to play. All African leaders agree that the Press must play a part in nation-building. What is in dispute is how this part should be played.

The newspaper Press, in whatever country, is first and foremost a commercial undertaking. However altruistic, nationalistic or chauvinistic we pretend or claim to be, we must never lose sight of this in discussions about the role of the Press in the new states. All newspapers inform, educate, entertain and provoke discussion by carrying in their columns the news of the day, local and from farther afield; newspapers also carry editorial opinions on matters of public interest. Differences between newspapers arise from their choice of contents and how these contents are presented to the readers; these differences come about because of the prejudices, background, training and political bias or inclination of those who own or produce the newspapers. This is as it should be. It will be a very dull world indeed if all the newspapers in the world were to treat all news in the same way and carry identical editorial opinions on every public issue.

In the new states of Africa it has become almost a daily routine to 'bundle-out' newspaper reporters for printing inaccurate reports about events. This has become a sort of pastime of African politicians, and the charges made against

104

the offending journalists range from 'spying' to 'indulging in subversive activities, carrying false reports calculated to undermine the integrity or solidarity of the State'; or sometimes there are no charges at all. Behind this popular but annoying game of 'bundling-out' of reporters lies the dilemma facing African politicians and journalists: What role should the Press play in nation-building? The resolution of this dilemma is of the utmost importance, not only to the Governments of the new nations, the public and the newspaper proprietors and readers but also to the journalists who produce the newspapers.

Several philosophies have been propounded about the role of the Press in the new nations.

Under the Nkrumah regime, when Ghana pretended to be leading Ghanaians and all African states on the path of socialism towards union continental Government, the President issued a number of directives about the role of the Press in the new Africa. In his address to a conference of African Journalists on November 11, 1963, Nkrumah described the role of the Press in these words:

> 'Through the pages of African newspapers written by the pens of African journalists let the people read of the great deeds of our continent which made African Unity . . . imperative and of the greatest urgency; let them read and learn of the advantages . . . of central direction and planning not only of the political affairs of the continent but the economies as well. Let them learn about socialism as it is being interpreted for the first time in an African State—Ghana. This is a vital job for the Press.'[1]

The *Ghanaian Times* of October 25, 1962, laid down what must be described as the militant role of the Press in the new Africa in these words:

> 'The African journalist is fully conscious of the responsibility that rests on the shoulders of Africa's new journalists— that of keeping the people informed of the new developments in the country, the continent and the world; exposing imperialism and neo-colonialist machinations, projecting the African

personality and contributing to the African liberation struggle and building of African unity.

'The new African journalist keeps cheap sensationalism out of his duties and lays emphasis on the positive things that go to help in building the new Africa—does not relish the stories which do no credit to the advancement and education of the people.'[2]

Barely three weeks after the *Ghanaian Times* printed the above, Mr Lawrence R. Abavana, then Minister of Information and Broadcasting, propounded what could be described as the objective role of the Press in the new states in a speech to Ghanaian journalists at Achimota School:

'Criticism is the prerogative of the Press. The Press should not be a vehicle for character assassination, nor for boosting up selfishly one's personality. It should not indulge in unwarranted attacks on individuals, institutions and nations. It should not be a medium for settling individual differences, nor for seeking redress for individual wrongs. It is the responsibility of the Press to ensure that it does not become a dangerous instrument, confusing the people and distorting facts.'[3]

The militant and objective roles of the Press were laid down in Ghana at a time when the disbanded CPP was carrying out a witch-hunting campaign against certain Ministers and individuals in their own party. It is interesting to note the differences in approach to the Press outlined by the *Ghanaian Times* and that of the Minister for Information and Broadcasting.

In the radical states and even some of the moderate states where the newspapers are state-owned and controlled, editors arrogate to themselves the role of the policeman, prosecutor, judge, jury, jailer and executioner, all in the holy names of African socialism, national solidarity and African unity. Some of these editors go as far as laying down the law as to what is news, how it should be written, presented and interpreted to the reading public.

Any journalist who disagrees with this type of editorial decree is branded as a 'traitor, a CIA agent, imperialist stooge and a reactionary'. Such 'traitors' to the African cause are hounded out of jobs, jailed or socially ostracised, if they are nationals of the country; if not, 'bundled-out' of the country on the next available plane. These militant editors, of course, have the full backing of their Governments or some individuals in position of power who can and do lay down the law in Press matters. These are the propagandists for the *status quo*. In their propagandistic roles, such editors cannot help but abandon their true convictions as journalists. In their enthusiasm to serve their employers, they unconsciously become melodious pipers for their paymasters. They also equate the state with their country's ruling political party, and conveniently forget that the state includes all citizens, even members of dissident minority parties, if any.

The usual result of this militancy is that a curtain of fear and silence descends on the Press. The ordinary citizens develop tolerance for only the orthodox point of view on world affairs and intolerance for new or different approaches. Since orthodoxy has always been the stronghold of the *status quo*, The Enemy of New Ideas, Ideas that are Disturbing, those who are wedded to the orthodox view are isolated from the challenge of new facts.

This fear drives more and more men and women in all walks of life either to silence or into the folds of the orthodox. This fear is mounting and is breeding other fears— fear of losing one's job, fear of being investigated, fear of being detained without trial. And this fear stereotypes the thinking of the citizens, narrows the range of free public discussion and drives thoughtful people to despair.

In the moderate state where journalists operate objectively, they do their best to report what they believe to be the facts without let or hindrance. They believe that mankind's right to knowledge and the free use thereof should be enjoyed by their readers without 'doctoring' the news to suit the whims and caprices of politicians who naturally prefer to have the sugar without the vinegar. In such countries the newspapers do their best, according to their limited resources—human and financial—to uphold the banner of impartiality. Editors on good newspapers in such countries draw the line between news and views by keeping them separate in their columns. Such editors constantly keep in mind the teachings of the great C. P. Scott of the *Manchester Guardian*:

'The newspaper is of necessity something of a monopoly, and its first duty is to shun the temptation of monopoly. Its primary object is the gathering of news. At the peril of its soul, it must see that the supply is not tainted. Neither in what it gives nor in the mode of presentation, must the unclouded face of truth suffer wrong. Comment is free, facts are sacred. Propaganda, so-called, by this means is hateful. The voice of opponents, no less than of friends, has a right to be heard.'[4]

In the numerous one-party states of Africa it is superfluous, if not dangerous, to say that the views of opponents must be heard, since they are supposed not to exist. Nevertheless, it is important for a good newspaper to remember that comment must also be justly subject to a self-imposed restraint. It is well to be frank. It is better to be fair. A daily newspaper that does not disseminate truth is a cup of poison sent round every morning or afternoon to debilitate the life of the people.

The Press in the new states of Africa suffers from many inhibitions because of the extra-sensitivity of those in Government, both politicians and civil servants. Governments of these new states, for political reasons, are anxious to put only their best foot forward. They are thus easily offended when uncomplimentary reports are published about their policies or doings, however fair such reports may be.

African politicians resent 'false reports' of foreign journalists to whom they prefer to give interviews at the expense of their own national journalists. This paradox is the more baffling when one remembers that the same foreign journalists the politicians patronise publish more unfavourable reports about them than their own native journalists. The result is bad blood between journalists and politicians generally.

This bad relationship between politicians and journalists can only have detrimental effects on good government, and on what the public read and think about the Governments. It is the duty of Governments to explain their actions and policies to the public so that a reasonable number of informed citizens can follow what the Governments are trying to do. This duty is not made easier by the lackadaisical attitude of some Governments.

Lord Poole, former Vice-Chairman of the British Conservative Party, said of this problem:

> 'Far the most important aspect is the behaviour of the leading politicians themselves and the attitude of the political journalists. Leading politicians seem to tend to want only to see journalists when they want to make use of them. If they want to explain something to them, all too often the underlying reason is not that they are fulfilling their duty to inform the press and public, but only to try and get a good press.
>
> 'Alternatively, sometimes politicians tend to cultivate journalists with a good deal of insincerity in the hope that their demonstration of friendship will lead to a gentle press if not friendly treatment. Journalists, particularly political journalists, are far too experienced and, indeed, too cynical, to be taken in, in this way. Very few politicians are let down by experienced journalists or lobby correspondents. The truth is that most, if not all, politicians are frightened of the press, and most political journalists despise a good many politicians.'[5]

In the new states where politicians have sworn to cling to power, come rain or shine, Lord Poole's observations are so apt that only the purblind would challenge them.

Under these conditions what can the African journalist do to present his readers with a true or even a fair picture of what is happening in his country without adulterating his profession, without descending into the treacherous abyss of propaganda, without making enemies of the politicians and without losing his job? In short, what can he do to play an honourable role in the nation-building effort in the field in which he is qualified?

There are no easy answers to these questions. Each journalist must find the answers for himself.

However, even the most ambitious politicians and the most cynical journalists accept certain preconditions under which any newspaper must operate. Editors and journalists must remember that the Press has a responsibility to the public, even though it is a commercial concern. The Press has a right to probe and demand answers it considers are in the public interest. It should be the duty of the Press in the new states of Africa to air openly public views and discussions on matters of policy without fear or favour of politicians, provided they do so within the laws of the various countries.

It is in the interest of the new states of Africa that the Press should be allowed to present the news without bias, interpret it objectively, without pandering to the whims and caprices of those in power, advertisers, and other pressure groups. African politicians shout unceasingly that the 'eyes of the world are on us'; that 'the world is watching what Africans will do with their new-found freedom', that 'the African states are on trial'. These expressions are the meaningless wailings of men suffering from inferiority complexes. These are the wailings of politicians who have not yet learnt the Sophoclean lesson that 'nothing tests the quality of people more than the exercise of authority'. What matters after independence is not what foreigners say about us, but our own integrity and ability to use power wisely. By this alone shall the African leaders be judged.

This is one aspect of independence in which the Press in the new nations can play a vital role. If African journalists would always remember that their countries are now free and independent, and that they can make their own newspapers worthy of this freedom by not seeing imperialist and neo-colonialist plots under every blade of grass, in every phrase carried in the overseas Press about their countries, they would be rendering a service of incalculable value, first to their own profession and secondly to their compatriots in the dissemination of information and views.

African newspapers must have their own correspondents in the capitals of neighbouring states and in other capitals overseas, but in fact very few have. The result is that African newspapers depend on the news agencies of foreign countries for the coverage of African news. However fair these foreign news agencies are, they are bound to present a biased picture of African events simply because 'not knowing our problems, they see not through our eyes'.

African states must improve their lines of communication between their capitals. Telecommunications links between African countries are notoriously inefficient because of our colonial past. The efforts being made by the Economic Commission for Africa to link the various African countries in this field must be speeded up so that contacts can be established with African capitals direct without going through Europe.

African states must also improve their internal transportation system to enable easy and efficient distribution of newspapers.

These are some of the problems facing the African Press. Some of them must be solved before the Press can begin to play a really effective role in nation-building in the new states.

After the February 24, 1966, revolution in Ghana, almost every public speech made by leading Ghanaians contained an appeal to the Press to help build the nation. Most intellectuals blame the Ghana Press for contributing to the dictatorship of the Nkrumah regime. Yet most of these very intellectuals have conveniently forgotten that they themselves were the principal collaborators of the ousted regime.

The Ghana example shows that however backward the Press may be, the new leaders of Africa expect it to play an important role in their nation-building efforts. The Press cannot play this role if it is gagged, pushed around by politicians, and above all, if it is owned by the state and controlled by some misguided politicians who expect it to play a melodious tune all the time because they pay the piper. Such paymasters perhaps forget that even the best pipers are sometimes compelled by circumstances to play discordant notes. Nation building is a co-operative effort. No one particular institution of the state can be expected to shoulder all the responsibility.

The African Press of the future must become an educated organ if it hopes to play any part in the exciting nation-building adventure. An educated Press can become an efficient instrument for the dissemination of information, education, for provoking discussion and stimulating ideas. The time has passed when journalism must be considered only as a passport to drinking and wining with the noble and ignoble, the accused and the innocent, the greats and the near-greats in Africa. Time is coming when the ignorant pedlar of well-worn clichés will have no place in the newspaper offices in the new Africa. Time is coming when the ordinary reader will begin to question some of the false assumptions which are now taken for granted. Time will come when newspaper readers will realise that politicians cannot provide them with prefabricated solutions to their national problems. When that time comes, only efficient journalists and honest politicians will survive to play an honourable role in the great adventure of nation-building in the new Africa.

9
Communism in Africa

THE PACE OF change in Africa today is so fast that the individual is becoming increasingly conscious of being on the run in trying to keep up with it. The pressure of population, the ever-present danger of famine, the threat of thermonuclear war and the insistent demand for social justice are four of the principal forces militating against freedom and driving African leaders toward totalitarianism. These forces are driving governments of various African countries toward regulation and regimentation. In the fields of economics, politics, the mass media of information and even in education, opportunities for exercising individual freedom are rapidly diminishing.

These are some of the developments that have made our age unique. But our African situation is not unique in being unique. Other periods in human history have also been unique in their own way. What is unique about the African situation is that it portrays vividly the nightmare of George Orwell's '1984', that without freedom man would no longer be human.

We noted at the beginning of this book that nationalism is one of the many faiths that spearheaded the African revolution after World War II; that it was the leadership of ardent African nationalists that made possible the liquidation of imperialism and colonialism on the continent; and that it was the same nationalist leaders who promised their countrymen and women 'pie in the sky' after the attainment of independence. We also noted that Africa faces, perhaps, a decade of turmoil, revolution and *coups d'état* before many of the new states can even begin to meet or remotely satisfy the famous 'rising expectations' of their teeming millions.

It is relevant in this situation to mention the fact that nationalism is not the only pebble on the African revolutionary beach. Other faiths as potent as, and even more pervasive than, nationalism are shaping the course of events in developing Africa today. These faiths include Catholic and Protestant Christianity, Islam and secular Communism. Except for Communism, all the faiths believe in the sacredness of the personality of the individual and also give the individual human being effective spiritual help in leading his personal life. Western historians equate the teachings of these faiths with the Western way of life, which places a high value on individual personality. Secular Communism and other totalitarian faiths, on the other hand, maintain that the individual human being exists for the sake of the community, as the ant exists for the sake of the ant-heap and the bee for the sake of the beehive. Communism today is effectively challenging the ancient religions for the allegiance of the underprivileged peoples in most developing countries and effectively undermining the ancient attitudes of these peoples toward their societies and way of life.

In Africa, as elsewhere, Communism has presented itself as the only sincere ally of nationalism. Through propaganda, slogans, aid programmes, foreign policy pronouncements and smooth diplomacy, the Soviet and Chinese Governments are desperately trying to penetrate the African continent by their identification with African leaders and by equating Communism with nationalism, anti-colonialism and anti-neocolonialism. The temptation to accept the blandishments of Communism is very attractive because the unsophisticated are easily persuaded that the Communists have all the answers; they do sincerely believe that through the application of Communist methods to their economic problems they can find a short-cut toward development and catch up with the West in material efficiency and power. This belief is predicated on the argument that what the 'backward' Russians were able to achieve within a short space of fifty years —since the Bolshevik revolution of November, 1917—they too could do in Africa, and perhaps do faster by avoiding some of the obvious mistakes of the Soviet Communists.

Classical Marxism appeals to only very few African intellectuals. Lenin's adaptations of the Marxist hypothesis, particularly the extension of the theory of the class struggle beyond national boundaries, however, have tremendous appeal to some African leaders who are avid for power and domination over their own nations. Such leaders and the new class of the educated élite use Communism principally as a political instrument to achieve and keep power. In the field of economics, Communism appeals to the younger generation of the educated élite who erroneously believe that the application of Communism to their intractable and apparently insoluble problems of development—problems aggravated by poverty, disease, ignorance and apathy—will enable them to telescope twenty centuries of Western technological achievement into a single decade. These are the young visionaries who would like to fly before they have learnt to crawl.

How is Communism faring in the new African states? How large is the membership of this secular faith which is even now disintegrating in the homeland of Communism itself? What methods have the Communists used to seduce the unsophisticated and what prospects have Communist parties of gaining effective political power in the new Africa?

These questions must be asked and answered because of the tremendous impact of this new faith on the peoples of Africa. The Communists have, through concerted propaganda, economic aid, training of young Africans and activities at the United Nations and elsewhere, impressed a large number of Africans and proclaimed their faith as the hope of the future. How far is this claim true and how will it affect the future of Africans in all parts of the continent tomorrow?

Prior to independence, very few Africans ever heard of Communism, much less were attracted to its teachings. The few Africans who had any contacts at all with the Communists were African students in Western European universities and a few adventurous African trade unionists like President Sekou Touré of Guinea who received some training in the Soviet Union. During the struggle for independence British colonial administrators made a sad mistake by describing all nationalist agitators as Communists. In the Gold Coast for example, it was the arrest of the 'Big Six' of the United Gold Coast Convention and the false label of Communists attached to them by the British colonial administration that introduced the word Communism into Gold Coast political vocabulary in 1948.

It is true, however, that most of the current leaders of Francophone Africa have had some contacts with the French Communist party in their student days in Paris and elsewhere in France. Today very few of them could be described as ardent Communists or even fellow travellers. There are exceptions like President Touré who describes himself as a 'Marxist revolutionary' and ex-President Nkrumah of Ghana who calls himself a 'Marxist socialist'.

Today, revolutionary communism is seeking to insert itself into the evolution of Africa because of six factors, namely nationalism, the policy of neutralism or non-alignment, the emotional issues of anti-colonialism and anti-neo-colonialism, egalitarianism, the prevalent ideas of socialism and the need for rapid development. The revolutionary communists of the Soviet Union, Eastern Europe and their Chinese colleagues from the Far East have all used some or all facets of these emotional issues to find a foothold on the African continent in an endeavour to control the peoples through political, cultural, economic and diplomatic contacts and pressures.

Africans today do not regard nationalism as a mere political instrument. Nationalism has found expression in race consciousness or pride in the African personality. President Leopold Senghor of Senegal and his disciples call this race consciousness negritude, and have, through their writings, generated a new pride in the African race. Nationalism transcends national boundaries by promoting Pan-Africanism or continental solidarity, a concept which led to the birth of the Organisation for African Unity. In some areas of the continent, nationalism expressed in tribal or sectional solidarity has led to secessionist movements or demands for tribal or regional autonomy. Classical examples of this type of nationalism in recent years are the Katanga secessionist movement in 1960, the Simba rebellion in the Kwilu and Kivu Provinces of the Congo-Kinshasa in 1964, and the Biafran secession of Ibo tribesmen in the Federal Republic of Nigeria in 1967.

Although nationalism, expressed either as national political weapon, tribal, regional or continental solidarity, leaves no room for international Communism, the Communists have nevertheless tried to use it as a convenient weapon to intervene in African affairs. Communist arms were sent to the *Simbas* of Pierre Mulele in the Congo and other dissident forces elsewhere in Africa for use against their own governments.

Communism appeals to African nationalists who are fighting either against their national governments or against the remaining colonialist regimes in Africa. During the struggle for Algerian independence, both the Soviet Union and Communist China sent large stocks of arms and war *materiel* to the Algerian freedom fighters. The freedom fighters in Mozambique, Angola and Portuguese Guinea and the Zimbabwe nationalists of Rhodesia today receive military hardware from the Communist countries to help them 'biff out' the colonial regimes in their countries. For these freedom fighters, there is no question of choice. The Communist regimes in Eastern Europe and China are the only governments that would send them arms to fight against their colonial masters. This is good enough reason for them to be attracted to Communism.

The polarisation of international affairs after World War II left the newly independent nations of Asia and Africa no choice in their conduct of international relations. Faced with this dilemma, some African countries following the lead of India under the late Prime Minister, Jawarharlal Nehru, adopted a policy of neutralism as the safest posture. In course of time it became clear, however, that these new nations could not possibly remain neutral in matters affecting their own destinies. Slowly but surely the new nations realised that their own national interests demanded that they make a choice, since the position of non-choice between the two giants in the Cold War was clearly absurd. A new policy of non-alignment was evolved, giving the leaders of the new nations freedom to choose the best of both systems.

But even under the policy of non-alignment our new leaders know consciously that they must fear the more aggressive side in any international dispute or argument. And the past record at the United Nations and elsewhere has shown that the Soviet Union and other Communist states are always the more aggressive side in these disputes. Thus it is that the so-called non-alignment of the African states leans heavily towards the East as we have already shown in an earlier chapter in this book. Our new leaders believe that they are safer under the umbrella of the Communist states when confronted with a choice between the two sides in the Cold War.

Anti-colonialism is perhaps the most emotional issue on the African continent today. During the struggle for independence many African leaders, particularly those from former Trusteeship territories, received a great deal of diplomatic and sometimes financial support from the Communist regimes of Eastern Europe and the Soviet Union. African leaders feel under an obligation, therefore, to support Communist policies at the United Nations and at other international gatherings as a pay-off for the support the Communist states gave them in yesteryears. This is another reason why Communism has such an attraction for some leaders.

Our African governments are passionately attached to the concept of egalitarianism as a primary goal. They believe that human dignity is impossible when you have second- and third-class citizens in society. This egalitarianism is expressed in strong opposition to the presence of delegates from the

Republic of South Africa and Portugal at international conferences because of the apartheid policy of the former and the assimilation policy of the latter. Our leaders believe genuinely that they can never be fully accepted into the comity of nations if South Africa and Portugal are allowed to get away with their racist policies and degrading treatment meted out to the citizens of the black race in their respective countries and territories.

In these arguments and demonstrations at international gatherings the African states can count always on the full and ready support of the Communist states. Our African leaders assume that the Communist states believe, as they themselves do, in human dignity, an attribute which apartheid South Africa and colonialist Portugal have denied them. The search for human dignity in all types of relations with other countries and prestige in international diplomacy are two other good and valid reasons why African leaders are attracted to the teachings of Communism.

Most African countries are still predominantly agricultural countries. Their subsistence economies are unorganised, undeveloped and chaotic in the extreme. Their only hope, many leaders believe, lies in quick industrialisation so that they can satisfy the 'rising expectations' of their people. In this quest for industrialisation several African countries have received enormous financial and technical aid and 'free' gifts from the Soviet Union, China and other Communist states.

Most African countries adopt African socialism as the most appropriate concept under which to solve their development problems. They find many similarities between their concept of African socialism and Communism and the teaching of Marx and Engels.

These goals or factors on the African scene provide good grounds for Communist penetration and attraction to Communism, but they also contain the seeds of opposition to Communism and the eventual disintegration of this secular faith.

While we have examined some of the factors on the African scene that make Communism attractive to some leaders and the younger generation of the élite, there is no evidence to suppose that Communism as a faith is on the ascendant in African countries or even that Communist parties will be in power in a large number of countries in the next decade. The evidence is that the total number of active or ardent Communists in the whole of Africa is not more than about 50,000. This evidence is an indication that the Communists have so far missed the political power boat not because of want of trying but because they entered the race for domination of the minds of the people late and also because their tactics have been very clumsy, crude and in some cases blatantly stupid in the past. This is so particularly in the case of the Chinese Communists whose arrogance and disdain for the African have made them anathema even to some ardent Communists in several African countries.

Communism as a faith is repugnant to a substantial cross-section of Africans in every country for various valid reasons. African intellectuals trained in Western and American universities and other institutions hate Communism. Some students trained in the very home of Communism, the Soviet Union, abhor it; politicians and leaders of most countries do not want to hear even the mention of the word. African farmers do not understand Communism and want no part of it because they do not see why they should toil and till the land for someone else while they themselves remain wage-earners until the end of time.

The independent market 'mammies' in Ghana have no wish to become Communists, not because they understand what Communism means but because their independence and affluence cannot co-exist with Communism. Political leaders in Kenya have hounded out Communist agents from their country because they abhor the atheism implicit in this secular faith; some Nigerian leaders look upon Communism with scorn because they consider it a fake religion designed to lure the faithful from the paths of reason and national advancement. African traditionalists hate Communism because its revolutionary nature disturbs the even tenor of their ways. Above all, most Africans hate Communism and want no part of it in their countries because of the Communists' perverse use of language and the semantic subversion characteristic of Communism.

Let us examine the performance of some African leaders and political parties that have closely imitated the Communist style of conducting business in Africa and find out how far their words have matched their actions. We hope this examination will make clear why some Africans abhor Communism.

The banned Convention People's Party of Ghana was not officially designed by its founders, general secretary and life chairman, Nkrumah, as a Communist party. Nkrumah, however, described himself as a Marxist socialist. This was the nearest he and his party theoreticians went in identifying themselves officially with Communism. The record of the CPP before assumption of power and for the fifteen years it remained in power, however, clearly demonstrated that it was a Communist party in everything but in name. And the evidence?

The CPP under Nkrumah was closely patterned on the Communist model of a political party; it used Communist methods of organisation—intimidation, blackmail, character assassination, deceit, rigged elections, single lists of election candidates, and every other trick from the Communist book to win and retain power and finally imposed a merciless dictatorship on Ghanaians.

A study of the CPP record in and out of power is a case history of Communist-style political operation in Africa and demonstrates how dangerous this type of political party can be.

The CPP presented itself to the people of Ghana as a party of the underdog, the 'vanguard of the proletariat' in a country with no proletariat, no capitalists and few industries. The CPP invoked Marxism to free its élite of moral inhibitions so that they could pursue power unhampered. Equally, they invoked Marxism, which they designated 'Nkrumah-ism', to justify their unceasing hostility to all persons and organisations outside the CPP and sanctioned aggression, thuggery and intimidation as moral and inevitable.

Nkrumahism, in fact, did not believe in the doctrine of the class struggle as defined by Marx and Engels, but it used it to mean the struggle between the CPP and other Ghanaian political parties, before and after independence, to eliminate political opposition.

The Spark, the theoretical organ of the CPP, in 1964 described intellectuals of Ghana as 'a backward-looking intellectual élite' and called for their destruction. This class includes all the professional men and woman such as lawyers, doctors, teachers, senior civil servants, judges, university lecturers, church leaders and experienced administrators. Under the CPP those intellectuals who did not conform or toe the party line were hounded out of the country, gaoled under the notorious Preventive Detention Act, disgraced or dismissed from their jobs without reason. They were replaced in most cases by what *The Spark* called the 'revolutionary proletariat', who believed unquestioningly in the cult of the personality of the Leader.

The CPP by its very nature—a mass political party covering the whole of Ghana—did not represent any particular class. It consisted simply of an élite of its own creation that entrenched itself in power. For this reason it was free to look for support from all manner of organisations like the Ghanaian Trades Union Congress, the farmers and co-operative societies, the women's organisations and market women, all of which it turned in course of time into integral wings of the party itself. This development was logical, since Communist parties do not tolerate the existence of rival political parties.

Communists always delude their unsuspecting converts that their system is more democratic and progressive than other totalitarian faiths such as fascism, and that Communists are engaged in a struggle between the rich and the poor, the haves and the have-nots, workers and employers, the oppressed and oppressors. Experience of the CPP and its record demonstrate beyond any reasonable doubt the fallacy of these claims.

The CPP in power was more repressive than the discarded colonial system for various reasons. One principal reason was that the CPP aimed at revolutionising Ghanaian society and therefore approached the question of economic and social development with a totalitarian mentality. The leaders of the party wanted everything and everybody in Ghana to come under the wing of the party. In this attempt at uniformity the party became a Big Brother without whose fiat no one could live a decent life. The CPP became not a party for the poor or a party engaged in bettering the conditions of poor Ghanaians but simply a party of a chosen élite in whom reposed all power. The leaders of this élite amassed great wealth for themselves while the masses were left destitute.

The CPP was able to win the support of Ghanaians in the urban areas at first, and later, through intimidation, economic pressures, blackmail and repressive legislation, was able to capture the whole of Ghana. Nkrumahism appealed to the urban population because they were the most alienated section of the community.

In every African country the minority of educated Africans who live in the urban centres are the most detribalised or alienated from their traditional authorities, values, morals and social organisation. These detribalised urbanites are the vectors of the famous 'revolution of rising expectations' and, therefore, most susceptible to the blandishments of Communism. So it was in Ghana when the propagandists of the CPP organised these urbanites and promised them manna from the skies.

It is from this class of frustrated urbanites that good material is recruited as the 'vanguard of the proletariat'. In Nigeria, the Socialist Workers Party was mainly composed of this type of detribalised Nigerian.

The late Okotie-Eboh, Nigerian Federal Minister of

Finance, perhaps spoke for a great number of Africans when he castigated the cant and humbug of the 'bearded doctors and chemists' of the Nigerian Socialist Workers Party and their alien type of socialism which they sought to import into Nigeria.

'The socialism preached by these false prophets,' he said, 'is an alien, imported heresy. But there is a true African philosophy, which I like to call indigenous communalism, and which I believe the leader of a major political party called pragmatic African socialism. This is very different from what I call socialism. It is deep-rooted in our way of life, related to our local conditions and concerned with practical optimum results for our national interests.

'This socialism or African reformist philosophy is in no way the same thing as deceitful revolutionary Marxist Communism, unmellowed by the experience of time and the peculiar circumstances of African society. Our African socialism is evolutionary, not revolutionary.'

In lighter vein, Okotie-Eboh ridiculed the Nigerian Socialist Workers Party leadership and predicted that when they too became affluent they would ride in big cars and shave off their beards and look respectable. In Ghana, most of the activists of the CPP kept their beards as a camouflage as they rode in their big shiny cars while their wasp-waisted 'masses' looked on with hunger gnawing at their intestines.

Africans dislike Communism because of Communist double-talk. While the Nkrumahists of Ghana were shouting 'African unity' from the roof-tops and pleading with neighbouring African countries to form a 'Union Continental Government now' the Nkrumah regime was systematically and secretly undermining these very regimes by training guerrilla fighters to overthrow governments which he did not consider sufficiently progressive and revolutionary.

The Nkrumah regime in Ghana demonstrated, like Communist regimes elsewhere, that Communists are neither reluctant to substitute military conquest or intervention (as in the Congo), subversion (as against Niger, etc.) and *coups d'état* (as in Togo) for the 'proletarian revolution' they preach, nor do they hesitate to impose a tiny élite of intellectual freebooters (as in the large number of foreign Communists at Nkrumah's Court) for the working masses whom the regime pretended to represent.

Africans also abhor Communism because religion is deeply ingrained in the social fabric. The monotheistic religions of Islam and Christianity, which give a truer insight into the nature of deity and its relation to man and modern technology, which give a more realistic understanding of the nature of inanimate objects and their use of men, appeal more to the African than atheistic Communism which describes religion as an 'opium' for the toiling masses. Communism also confuses the material and the spiritual as much as did the animist religions of ancient Africa. To many Africans the invitation being extended to them by Communist propagandists is an invitation to backwardness and a life without religion.

I personally do not believe, as some others do, that the future in Africa belongs to Communism. I believe that in the long run the shibboleths being shouted from the rooftops today by the Communists will simply become tomorrow's headstones for yesterday's issues, particularly when colonialism is completely liquidated on our continent. New issues will arise, but these issues will be solved through practical commonsense and not through adherence to the teachings of an alien secular faith which is even now disintegrating before our very eyes.

The People and the Future

IN HIS *Prologue to African Conscience* the Ethiopian poet Tsegave Gabre Medhin saw the African dilemma in these words:

> *Shamed to bend*
> *Into the model chairs*
> *Carpentered for it*
> *By the friendly Pharaohs of its time*
> *The Black Conscience flutters*
> *Yet it is taken in*
> *It looks right,*
> *It looks left,*
> *It forgets to look into its own self.*[1]

In the Africa which we are trying to build for ourselves and our progeny we must never forget to look into our own self. Too often our leaders try to blame outside forces, such as neo-colonialism, neo-imperialism, the discriminatory trade prices and sharp commercial deals of the industrialised countries for many of our failures and backwardness. Blaming outside forces for our failures is true only up to a point. Our problems can be solved more efficiently if we but pause to conduct agonising self-criticisms and self-examinations to discover the right solutions.

We have seen the salesmen of both Western and Eastern 'democracies' spending a great deal of time and money in efforts to win the hearts of the new African states. Some of these salesmen have tried to impose their way of life on Africans because they are convinced that their way is the better way. Others, like the Soviet communists, have made plain their intentions. They are extending foreign aid to African states because they wish to capture and finally dominate the markets of Africa for the raw materials they can exchange for their manufactured goods. The Communist Chinese on the other hand want to use Africans to fight their 'socialist wars of liberation' for them. Lin Piao, Mao Tse-tung's heir apparent and Defence Minister, says:

'It is sheer day-dreaming for anyone to think that, since our revolution has been victorious, our national construction is forging ahead, our national wealth is increasing and our living conditions are improving, we too will lose our revolutionary fighting will, abandon the cause of world revolution and discard Marxism-Leninism and proletarian internationalism.'[2]

The Chinese believe that their mission is to wage 'wars of liberation' all round the world. And they plan to use the peoples of the under-developed countries as fodder in waging these wars. They have demonstrated in all their dealings with the new states of Africa their contempt for the African way of life and have strained all their resources to train African converts to carry out their plans for causing confusion on the continent. So far, they have made very little headway, not for want of trying but principally because many African leaders have seen through the Chinese game and have rejected the atheism implicit in communism.

We have seen that international communism, despite its extensive and intensive campaign, has failed thus far to win any substantial number of African converts. Yet the contest for the imposition of foreign ideological, political and economic solutions on Africa will continue. There is no prospect for a final defeat of communism in Africa if the conditions that favour communism remain: poverty, ignorance, disease and apathy.

Our current African leaders see the threat of communism in varied ways. President Felix Houphet-Boigny of the Ivory Coast and François Tombalbaye of Chad, for instance, see Chinese communism as a long-term threat and believe that it would penetrate the under-populated and poverty-stricken areas of the continent, using subversion, propaganda, sabotage and economic infiltration as its weapon to win the hearts of individuals, organisations and political parties.

President Julius Nyerere of Tanzania sees communism as just one of the alien forces contending for the allegiance of Africans.

President Kenneth Kaunda of Zambia wants his country to stay aloof from the ideological warfare, and wants no help from the opposing giants, the United States and the Soviet Union, but rather from the smaller countries, such as Israel and Canada, that are not committed to the Cold War.

President Jomo Kenyatta and his Government have decisively rejected the Chinese brand of communism and have thrown out many agents of Chinese and Eastern European communism.

To defeat the threat of communism on the continent African leaders must intensify their efforts to eliminate the conditions that favour communism. This they can do by providing the education, economic development projects and social services that alone can woo the peoples from the blandishments of the communists.

Another threat which militates against peace and political stability in Africa is the proliferation of one-party states. Many African leaders have been persuaded to accept the fiction that the one-party state is the only workable system that can ensure coherence, national solidarity and unity in the developing states of Africa. Our leaders have swallowed the propaganda of the communist agents and their Western allies that, in the backward states of Africa, the existence of opposition or minority parties is an expensive luxury which the new states afford at their own peril.

None of the eloquent arguments thus far advanced in support of the one-party state has stood the test of critical analysis. The protagonists forgot that there can also be unity in diversity, that members of minority or opposition parties are also nationals of their common country, and that members of such parties become malcontents only when they are ruthlessly suppressed and driven underground or put into detention camps without due process of law. The one-party state by its very nature is eminently discriminatory and dictatorial as has been proved in Ghana. It is patently false to assert, as a Ghana newspaper did on February 3, 1964, that those who vote against propositions of the ruling one-party state 'are automatically transformed into subversive elements and enemies of the people; dangerous criminals let loose in society'.[3]

In a mature society, the rulers of the moment must be tolerant enough to allow dissenting voices to be heard, however discordant such voices may be, if they pretend that they are practising democracy.

The greatest danger facing Africa today is our current rulers' intolerance of dissenting views. The political coup in Uganda in 1966, the stories of plots in various countries since Independence, the elimination and suppression of minority parties and their leaders from playing a part in nation-building efforts in various countries, all are manifestations of this intolerance of minority parties and the desire to do away with their criticisms and ideas. It is this same intolerance which has led to the vast corruption of ruling parties and their leaders in several countries and their desire to remain forever in power, no matter how unpopular they have become. It is this same intolerance which has led to the rigging of elections in many countries on our continent.

In imperial Rome, the policy of bread and circuses was not enough to disguise from the public the state of corruption and inefficiency, above all when bread became scarce. Ghana could not escape the same fate under the Nkrumah regime. Likewise, the developing nations of Africa cannot escape reality. There is a growing demand for justice and human dignity; there is growing demand for fair play, along with demands for economic and social progress. All our splendid monuments, beautiful projects, resonant slogans and grandiose dreams will not be sufficient to mask the disagreeable facts of life. Above all, the inordinate ambitions of our politicians to cling to power in face of the failures of their policies will not bring peace and stability.

Dr Azikiwe, former President of the Federal Republic of Nigeria, warned of the dangers of inordinate ambition, corruption and denial of human rights in December, 1964, when the politicians of his country began to tear the country apart. He said in a prophetic broadcast to his people:

'I am not quite happy at the political turn of events in our embryo republic. The way and manner our electioneering campaign is being conducted leaves much to be desired. It is no exaggeration to say that with regularity I have been receiving correspondence complaining of victimisation, privation, false imprisonment, malicious prosecution, denial of bail for trifling offences, beating of political opponents and refusal of permits to hold electioneering meetings.

'I have one advice to give our politicians: if they have decided to destroy our national unity then they should summon a round-table conference to decide how our national assets should be divided before they seal their doom.

'I make this suggestion because it is better for us and for our many admirers abroad that we should disintegrate in peace and not in pieces. Should politicians fail to heed this warning, then I will venture a prediction that the experience of the Democratic Republic of the Congo (Kinshasa) will be child's play if ever it comes to our turn to play such a tragic role.

'Nigeria has established a reputation as Africa's bastion of democracy and we should not allow inordinately ambitious politicians to disfigure our national image by their disreputable tactics. Unless their wings are clipped now our beloved country may be plunged into an avalanche of social unrest.'[4]

The tragedy of Nigeria and of Africa is that the 'disreputable'—and some not so disreputable—politicians of Nigeria did not heed Dr Azikiwe's warning. Exactly thirteen months to the day after his warning, Nigeria was plunged into a military *coup d'état*, which resulted in a horrible and tragic fratricidal war. Dr Azikiwe's warning is as germane today as it was in December, 1964. What Africans, the humble citizens in the rural areas, the villages and hamlets throughout the continent, desire above everything else are peace and stability so that they can live their lives in dignity. Can the politicians of Africa ensure their fellow countrymen the fulfilment of this simple desire? That is the challenge of today and tomorrow in Africa.

It is my belief that the future belongs to the people of Africa. I have faith in Africa and I believe that left to herself Africa can solve her problems in her own way. Africa needs peace, the friendly hand of aid of the peoples of both East and West to travel the adventurous road to economic prosperity, social progress and democracy. The peoples of both East and West can help if they refrain from imposing their ideologies on Africans, and if Africans themselves can develop their own concepts and find their own solutions. Africa can use the technological know-how of the advanced industrial nations. She can take advantage of all the benefits that modern science can bestow and profit by the experience of other nations. But to build a modern, prosperous and just society for Africans in Africa, the African must find his own soul.

The late Dr R. E. G. Armattoe in one of his poems expresses his faith in Africa in these words:

> *Come peace or come war,*
> *Come love, life or death,*
> *In splendid array and glamour*
> *I'll remain steadfast in my Faith.*[5]

So do the youth of Africa believe that the future belongs to them. They have faith in Africa's greatness.

Reference Notes
and Index

Reference Notes

CHAPTER ONE

1. *The New York Times*, International edition, May 9, 1966.
2. Busia, K. A. *Africa In Search of Democracy* (Routledge & Kegan Paul, London, 1967) page 25.
3. *Ashanti Pioneer*, August 14, 1957. Speech by Cecil M. Ford, at Accra West End Arena on August 13, 1957.
4. Nkrumah, Kwame, *Ghana*, Nkrumah's autobiography, frontispiece.
5. Friedland, W. H. & Rosberg, Jr, Carl G., *African Socialism* (Stanford University Press, 1964) page 246.

CHAPTER TWO

1. Friedland, W. H. & Rosberg Jr, Carl G., *African Socialism* (Stanford University Press, 1964) page 242.
2. *West Africa*, No. 2635, December 2, 1967, page 1549.
3. *Ibid*, page 1549.
4. *Ibid*, page 1550.
5. *Ibid*, page 1550.
6. Friedland, W. H. & Rosberg Jr, Carl G., *African Socialism* (Stanford University Press, 1964) page 240.

CHAPTER THREE

1. Republic of Kenya: *Sessional Paper No. 10 of 1963/65*, para 4.
2. Republic of Kenya: *House of Representatives*, Official report, February 15, 1966, column 970.
3. *Ibid*, column 926.
4. *Ibid*, column 926–927.
5. Republic of Kenya: *The Revised Development Plan, 1966–1970* (Government Printer, 1966). Introductory chapter by President Jomo Kenyatta.

CHAPTER FOUR

1. Friedland, W. H. & Rosberg Jr, Carl G., *African Socialism*, (Stanford University Press, 1964) page 267–268.
2. *Ibid*, page 271.
3. *Ibid*, page 275.
4. Republic of Ghana: *The Proposals of the Constitutional Commission for a Constitution for Ghana* (State Publishing Corporation, 1968) page 190.
5. *Ibid*, page 191.
6. *Ibid*, pages 190–191.
7. Friedland, W. H. & Rosberg Jr, Carl G., *African Socialism*, (Stanford University Press, 1964) page 132–133.
8. *West Africa*, No. 2644, page 123.
9. *Ibid*, No. 2645, page 148.
10. *Ibid*, No. 2645, page 148.

CHAPTER FIVE

1. *Daily Graphic*, February 19, 1968, page 10.
2. *Ibid*, page 10.
3. Africa Confidential, 1966, No. 7, page 7.
4. *Ibid*, 1966, No. 15, page 7.
5. Kurt Muller: *The Foreign Aid Programs of the Soviet Bloc and Communist China: An analysis* (Walker & Company, New York, 1967), page 193.
6. *Ibid*, page 201.
7. *Ibid*, page 204.
8. *Ibid*, page 209.

CHAPTER SIX

1. *Daily Graphic*, October 20, 1966, page 5.

CHAPTER SEVEN

1. *Africa 1964*, No. 24.
2. *Daily Nation*, April 14, 1965.

CHAPTER EIGHT

1. *Evening News*, March 14, 1964.

2. *Ghanaian Times*, October 25, 1962.
3. *Daily Nation*, February 5, 1964 (quoted).
4. Quoted from Documentation Service of International Federation of Journalists, 1965.
5. *Ibid*, Vol. VIII-10 of March 6, 1965.

CHAPTER TEN

1. *The New York Times*, International edition, May 10, 1966.
2. *Daily Nation*, September 8, 1965.
3. *Evening News*, February 3, 1964.
4. *Daily Nation*, December 22, 1964.
5. Armattoe, R. E. G.: *Deep Down the Blackman's Mind* (Arthur H. Stockwell, Ltd., 1954) From the poem, *They Tell Me You Are True*, page 65.

Index

Kenya Government Sessional
Paper No. 10, 30–1, 39–40, 45
Kenyatta, President Jomo, of
Kenya, 32, 34, 37, 96, 128
Kikuyu, 36
Kumi, Ayeh,
Kivu Province of Congo, 117
Kivukoni College Address, 16,
22, 29
Kodachenko, A., 72
K.P.U., 33, 37
Kruschev, Nikita, 71–2
Kwilu, Province of Congo, 117

Lamco, 57
Legum, Colin, 54
Lenin, 115
Lenin Peace Prize, 77, 81
Liberia, 56–8, 81
Lumumba, Patrice, 85, 94
Lumumba, Patrice, Institute, 36

Madagascar, 69
Mahgreb Economic Community,
100
Malagasy States, 80
Malawi, 97
Mali, 56, 80, 81, 86, 87
Mao Tse Tung, 114
Marshall Plan, The, 60
Martin, Minister for External
Affairs (Canada), 71
Mauritania, 87
Marxist–Leninist Doctrines, 20,
115, 119, 122, 127
Mba, President Leon, of Gabon,
56
Mboya, Tom, 33–5, 38
Middleton, Drew, 9
Medhin, Tsegave Dabre, 113
Mobutu, President Joseph D., of
The Congo, 84–5, 87
Monrovia Group, 80, 81, 82, 84
Moran Dr Hugh, 71
Morocco, 81, 86, 91, 101

Mozambique, 95, 98, 117
Mulele, Pierre, 85, 117

NADECO, 51
National Liberation Council
(Ghana), 54, 55
National University (of Kenya),
41
Nehru, President Jawarlal, of
India, 123
Netherlands, 62
New York Times, 9
Niger, 80, 124
Nigeria, 23, 29, 33, 55, 70–1, 81,
105, 117, 120, 123, 130
Nkrumah, Dr Kwame, President
of Ghana, 11, 29, 32, 33, 49–
55, 80, 87, 89–91, 105, 111,
116, 121–5
Nkrumah, Dr Kwame, Institute
of, 36
Nyerere, President Julius, of
Tanzania, 16, 22, 28, 113

Organisation of African Unity
(OAU), 80–7, 88, 90–1, 96,
102, 117
Observer, The, 54
OCAM, 17
Odinga, Oginga, ex Vice-Presi-
dent of Kenya, 32–3, 36–7
OECD, 62
Okotie-Eboh, 123–4
Orwell, George, 119

Pan-Africanism, 19–20, 101
Piao, Marshall Lin, 127
Poole, Lord, 109
Portugal, 97–8, 119
Potekin, Professor I, I, 74
Press, The, 104–111
Preventive Detention Acts, 101,
122
Prologue to African Conscience,
126